Strength for the Veteran's Soul

Strength for the Veteran's Soul:
A 90-Day Devotional for Warriors Fighting Battles Seen and Unseen

Brian Smith

Strength for the Veteran's Soul is a devotional written for U.S. military veterans seeking courage, healing, and renewed spiritual strength through Scripture and faith.

First Edition — 2025

Printed in the United States of America

CROWN & SQUARE
PRESS LLC

This devotional is a work of Christian inspiration. It is not intended to replace pastoral counseling, professional mental-health care, or medical guidance. Veterans experiencing crisis or acute distress are encouraged to contact appropriate professionals or veteran support organizations.

First Edition, 2025
Printed in the United States of America

ISBN (Paperback): 979-8-9941739-0-9

Cover Design: Brian Smith & AI-Assisted Design
Author: Brian Smith

Foreword

(By the Author)

When I first put on the uniform, I had no idea how deeply military service would shape my life. I didn't understand how the discipline, the brotherhood, the long nights, the quiet fears, and the unexpected battles would stay with me long after I came home. I also didn't know how much I would need God—not just on the tough days in uniform, but on the quieter, heavier days afterward.

Like many veterans, I carried things I didn't talk about. Some were physical: fatigue, chronic issues, pain that lingered. Others lived in the mind and heart: memories that resurfaced without warning, seasons of discouragement, moments of loneliness, and the slow search for purpose after the mission changed.

Over the years, through many different seasons of life, as a husband, a father of three, a business owner, a church leader, and a follower of Christ, I discovered something I wish someone had told me earlier:

God doesn't retire His soldiers. He redeploys them.

Your identity didn't end when your time in service ended. Your usefulness didn't stop when the uniform came off. Your mission didn't disappear when life moved forward.

You are still called.
Still needed.
Still capable.
Still valuable in the Kingdom of God.

This devotional was written for you, the veteran who has fought battles few people understand, who has carried weight quietly, who has served faithfully, and who still wants to honor God in the life you're living today.

For 90 days, we will walk through Scripture, real struggles, military analogies, and reflections designed to strengthen your spirit, steady your heart, and remind you that God has never once left your side. You may feel tired, worn down, or unsure of your next step, but God is still leading you, shaping you, and preparing you for what comes next.

My hope is simple:
That these pages encourage you.
That they remind you of your worth.
That they point you toward the One who carries every burden, heals every wound, and commands every victory.

Thank you for your service. Both to your country and to Christ.

May this devotional renew your strength and help you walk boldly into the purpose God has for you.

Stand firm, brother.
Jesus is with you.

Brian Smith

U.S. Army Veteran
Follower of Christ
Husband, Father, Servant

Dedicated to every veteran who is still fighting
battles long after the uniform came off.

May these pages strengthen your soul.

Day 1: The Call to Courage

Scripture: *Have not I commanded thee? Be strong and of a good courage; be not afraid, neither be thou dismayed: for the Lord thy God is with thee whithersoever thou goest. Joshua 1:9*

There's a unique kind of courage veterans understand. It's not the absence of fear. It's stepping forward while fear whispers in the background. You learned this early, whether standing on the yellow footprints, rucking under the weight of what felt like a truck, or boarding that plane toward a place you'd only heard about on the news.

Courage was expected. Strength was demanded. But faith? That was a quieter companion. Too often used in emergencies only.

Joshua's moment wasn't that different. He wasn't handed a sword and told, "Good luck." God gave him a command backed by a promise: you won't face a single moment alone. As a veteran, that hits deep. You've known the isolation of long nights, the replaying of memories, the questions that surface when the world gets quiet. Yet God's command remains steady:

Be strong. Be courageous. Not because of who you are, but because of Who walks with you.

Today, take courage. Not the military version that relies on adrenaline and training, but the spiritual kind that leans into God's presence. He has never once left your side.

Prayer:
Lord, give me Your courage today. Remind me that I never face a battle without You beside me.

Call to Action:

What is one area of your life where you need to choose courage today?

_____

_____

_____

_____

_____

Day 2: The Weight You Carried

Scripture: *Cast thy burden upon the Lord, and he shall sustain thee: he shall never suffer the righteous to be moved. 1 Peter 5:7*

Every veteran remembers carrying something heavy. A pack, a weapon, gear that made you feel like you were sinking into the ground with every step. But the heaviest weights were almost never the physical ones.

Some burdens you didn't even pick up. They were handed to you:

Memories.
Responsibilities.
Expectations.
Failures.
Survivor's guilt.
The pressure to be strong for everyone else.

As years pass, those weights shift. For some veterans, it's sleepless nights. For others, it's chronic problems, like sinus issues that never healed right, sleep apnea that leaves you exhausted, anxiety that creeps in without warning, or the frustration of feeling worn down by your own body.

Here's the truth Scripture gives you: God never intended for you to carry any of it alone.

You don't have to be the pack mule of your own life. You don't earn God's love by pretending you're unbreakable.

Your burden is not too much for Him. Your worries aren't "weak." Your struggles don't make you less of a man.

Today, loosen your grip. Shift the weight off your shoulders. Let Him carry what was never meant to be yours.

Prayer:
Father, help me release the weight I've carried for too long. Teach me to trust You with the burdens I cannot handle.

Call to Action:

What burden will you hand over to God right now?

_____

_____

_____

_____

_____

Day 3: The Chain of Command

Scripture: *Trust in the Lord with all thine heart; and lean not unto thine own understanding. Proverbs 3:5*

In the military, clarity matters. You knew who you reported to, who they reported to, and what the mission required. A good chain of command kept things functioning when chaos hit. A broken one put lives at risk.

In civilian life, the world tells you that *you* are the chain of command. Handle it yourself. Figure out your own path. Tough it out. Trust your instincts only.

But faith works differently.
Faith requires surrender.
Faith requires trust.
Faith places God at the top of the chain, not as a distant commander, but as a Father who leads with wisdom and love.

It's hard for veterans to release control. You've been trained to rely on skill, awareness, discipline. Letting God lead feels like breaking procedure. Yet Scripture calls you to a deeper kind of trust, one rooted not in understanding everything, but in believing that God already does.

Your life, your family, your health struggles, your calling, your future, belongs under His authority. Not to restrict you, but to free you.

Today, submit your plans, your worries, your decisions to the One who sees the whole battlefield.

Prayer:
Lord, take command of my steps today. Help me trust Your leadership more than my own understanding.

Call to Action:

Where do you need to trust God's leadership instead of your own understanding?

_____

_____

_____

_____

_____

Day 4: The Fog of War

Scripture: *For God is not the author of confusion, but of peace, as in all churches of the saints.*
1 Corinthians 14:33

Every service member learns quickly that not every battle is clear. Sometimes the hardest moments come with uncertainty. When visibility is low, intel is incomplete, and decisions must be made anyway. You move forward even when you can't see the whole picture.

Life after service isn't much different. There are days when the path ahead is foggy. Health issues cloud your strength. Fatigue fogs your mind. Anxiety shadows your confidence. Responsibilities pile up until everything feels blurry.

But God promises something powerful: He is not the author of confusion.

If there is fog in your life, it's not coming from Him.

Peace doesn't mean everything becomes easy. It means everything becomes clear. God cuts through the fog, not always by removing it, but by giving you enough clarity to take the next step.

You don't walk blindly.
You walk behind a Shepherd who sees through every clouded moment.

Prayer:
Lord, bring clarity to the foggy places in my life. Calm my mind and guide my steps with Your peace.

Call to Action:

What confusing situation do you need to ask God to clarify?

_____

_____

_____

_____

_____

Day 5: Situational Awareness

Scripture: *Be sober, be vigilant; because your adversary the devil, as a roaring lion, walketh about, seeking whom he may devour. 1 Peter 5:8*

Veterans learn to read a room in seconds. You've walked into unfamiliar places, sized up the atmosphere, and known right away when something felt "off." You learned how to notice the small things, body language, tone shifts, unusual movements, details others walk right past. That hyper-awareness once kept you alive. Even now, long after the uniform hangs in the closet, it can feel like something you can't fully turn off.

But spiritually, that same instinct is not a burden, it's a strength.

Scripture calls believers to stay alert and to stay awake. Not paranoid. Not fearful. Not constantly bracing for disaster. But aware. Watchful. Discerning. The enemy rarely storms through the front door shouting. More often, he works quietly, slipping in through small compromises, whispered discouragement, or subtle lies that sound almost true.

Your military training gave you a gift: you know how to maintain vigilance without losing peace.
Not anxious. Not jumpy. Just ready.

Today, put that awareness to work in a new way. Pay attention to the places where temptation might be hiding. Notice the moments when discouragement tries to take root. Listen closely for the gentle nudges of the Holy Spirit, those prompts to speak, to pray, to act, or simply to hold your ground.

You've faced battles that required more courage than what stands before you today. The same discipline that once kept you safe can now help guard your heart, your mind, and your walk with God.

You are trained. You are equipped.
And you are not fighting alone.

Prayer:
God, sharpen my awareness. Help me see the enemy's tactics and recognize Your guidance.

Call to Action:

What spiritual threat or temptation do you need to stay alert to today?

_____

_____

_____

_____

_____

Day 6: The Barracks Brotherhood

Scripture: *Iron sharpeneth iron; so a man sharpeneth the countenance of his friend.   Proverbs 27:17*

You never forget the people you served with. Even if you haven't seen them in years, there's a bond forged in sweat, discipline, and the unknown. You trained together. Complained together. Pushed each other through the worst days.

That kind of camaraderie is rare.

In civilian life, many veterans experience a painful loneliness. The closeness is gone. The shared mission is gone. The structure is gone. And sometimes, even faith can feel like a solo battle.

But God never designed you to walk alone.
You still need brothers. You still need sharpening.

Fellowship isn't weakness. It's a force multiplier.

Seek out strong Christian mentorship. Build relationships. Join a group. Attend Bible study. Reach out to someone who may be struggling silently.

The camaraderie doesn't end when the uniform comes off. It simply shifts to a new battlefield.

Prayer:
Lord, send strong brothers into my life and help me be a source of strength to them as well.

Call to Action:

Who is one person you need to reach out to for connection or encouragement?

_____

_____

_____

_____

_____

Day 7: Mission Focus

Scripture: *Wherefore seeing we also are compassed about with so great a cloud of witnesses, let us lay aside every weight, and the sin which doth so easily beset us, and let us run with patience the race that is set before us.*
Hebrews 12:1

Every mission has three essential elements: the objective, the obstacles, and the drive to keep going until the work is done. During your service, you pushed through heat, exhaustion, lack of sleep, and pain because the mission mattered. You understood the weight of responsibility, and you gave your best to see it through.

Life now has its own missions, just not the kind written on briefing papers:

Loving your family with patience and presence.
Serving your church with humility and heart. Guiding your children or those you influence toward truth and character.
Honoring God daily in the quiet choices no one else sees.
Growing into the person He designed you to become, step by step.

But mission drift is real. Distractions slip in unnoticed.
Fatigue makes even simple tasks feel heavy.
Discouragement whispers that it's easier to settle, easier to coast, easier to lose sight of your purpose.

That's why the writer of Hebrews speaks directly to the battle-tested heart: *run with endurance.*
Not with overwhelming speed.
Not with flawless perfection.
Endurance.

Endurance is steady. It is faithful. It is choosing to rise each day and take the next step, even when that step feels small or the path feels long. You don't need to conquer every challenge today. You simply need to keep moving forward with a willing spirit.

God provides the strength. You bring the willingness. Together, that's enough.

Your mission is not something left behind in the past.
It is not finished, forgotten, or over.
It is right in front of you, inviting you to take the next faithful step.

Prayer:
Father, help me stay focused on the mission You've given me. Strengthen my endurance to keep moving forward.

Call to Action:

What distraction do you need to set aside so you can stay focused on your mission?

_____

_____

_____

_____

_____

Day 8: Gear Check

Scripture: *Put on the whole armour of God, that ye may be able to stand against the wiles of the devil.*
Ephesians 6:11

Before stepping into danger, you checked your gear. Not once. Not casually. But consistently and with intention. You knew your life, and the lives of others, could depend on your readiness. You never stepped outside the wire unprepared, because preparation was part of survival.

Spiritually, God calls you to that same level of readiness.

The armor of God isn't symbolic, poetic, or optional. It's essential equipment for anyone who follows Christ, especially for those who know what it means to live with a target on their back.

Truth: keeps you grounded when confusion tries to pull you off course.
Righteousness: protects your heart from compromises that look harmless at first.
Peace: steadies your steps when chaos rises around you.
Faith: shields you from the lies the enemy whispers at your weakest moments.
Salvation: reminds you who you are and whose you are.
The Word: arms you for battle, giving you strength, clarity, and direction.

Leave one piece behind, and you feel it.
One gap becomes a weakness.
One missing layer of protection creates an opening the enemy is eager to exploit.

Many veterans walk into spiritual battles unprotected because they're used to relying on discipline, training, grit, and sheer determination. Those qualities served you well in uniform, but spiritual warfare is different. It isn't fought with muscle, willpower, or toughness. It requires spiritual equipment. God's equipment.

So today, take a moment for a spiritual gear check:

Where are you unprotected?
What part of your armor needs attention, repair, or reinforcement?
Which piece have you neglected without realizing it?

Suit up.
You've worn armor before. Now wear the kind that protects your soul.

You are a soldier of the Kingdom, and your readiness matters.

Prayer:
Lord, help me put on every piece of Your armor today. Prepare me for whatever battle I face.

Call to Action:

Which piece of God's armor do you most need to "put on" today?

_____

_____

_____

_____

_____

Day 9: The Long March

Scripture: *And let us not be weary in well doing: for in due season we shall reap, if we faint not.*
Galatians 6:9

Ask any veteran about a long march and they'll smirk, because every long march has three parts: the start (full of confidence), the middle (full of regret), and the finish (full of relief).

Life imitates the march.

The beginning of a dream feels exciting. The end goal feels rewarding. But the middle, the long, tiring, discouraging middle, is where most people quit.

If you feel stuck today…
If your body hurts…
If your spirit feels worn out…
If life feels like an endless, heavy march…

Take heart. God sees your endurance. He honors your perseverance. The finish line is ahead, even if you can't see it yet.

Don't quit in the middle.
You've been strengthened for the long haul.

Prayer:
God, renew my strength today. Help me keep marching even when the journey feels heavy.

Call to Action:

What is one step you can take to keep moving forward?

_____

_____

_____

_____

_____

Day 10: Firewatch Faith

Scripture: *My soul waiteth for the Lord more than they that watch for the morning: I say, more than they that watch for the morning. Psalm 130:6*

Every veteran remembers firewatch or guard duty, those long, quiet hours when you protected what mattered while others slept. The world felt different in those moments. The air was still, the darkness seemed heavier, and every sound echoed a little louder than usual. The minutes crawled, and fatigue tugged at your eyes, but you stayed awake because the mission required your alertness. Others were counting on you.

Faith has its own version of firewatch.

There are seasons when you're praying without hearing an answer. Seasons when you're waiting for direction but everything feels unclear. Times when you're standing guard over your family, your home, your calling, or your spiritual health while the rest of the world moves on as if nothing important is happening at all.

Those spiritual nights can feel long, longer than any shift you ever pulled. You can feel alone. You can feel weary. You can wonder if anything is changing in the darkness.

But just like the watchman waits for dawn, you wait with expectation, not despair. Morning always comes. God always moves. No night lasts forever. His timing is perfect, and His light breaks through at exactly the right moment.

Your task isn't to force the sunrise. It isn't to solve everything in the dark. Your job is simply to stay faithful,

to keep watch, keep praying, keep trusting, until the light breaks through and God reveals what He has been doing all along.

You've stood the night before.
With God beside you, you can stand this one too.

Prayer:
Lord, give me the strength to keep watch in faith, trusting that Your dawn is coming.

Call to Action:

What prayer will you stay faithful in today, even if the answer hasn't come yet?

_____

_____

_____

_____

_____

Day 11: Battle Fatigue

Scripture: *He giveth power to the faint; and to them that have no might he increaseth strength. Isaiah 40:29*

Military fatigue is more than tired legs. It's tired bones. Tired nerves. Tired spirit. It's the kind of exhaustion that sinks deep into you, the kind you push through because you have to, not because you have anything left to give. In uniform, you learned to function while exhausted, to complete the mission even when your body protested. But the weariness didn't always leave when the mission did.

Many veterans carry a form of battle fatigue long after their service ends.

Sleep that never feels refreshing. Anxiety that drains emotional and physical energy. Chronic pain in knees, hips, or old injuries that never fully healed. Exhaustion that lingers even after a full night's rest. The slow grind of feeling worn down in ways others may never notice.

These burdens are real. They take a toll. And some days, simply getting through the day feels like another mission in itself.

But God offers something no amount of sleep, caffeine, or determination can provide: renewal.

Not quick relief that fades overnight. Not a burst of motivation that disappears with the next wave of fatigue. But deep, sustaining strength that reaches places human endurance can't touch.

You may feel exhausted today. You may feel outmatched by what stands in front of you. You may feel like the battle is bigger than the energy you have left.

But God promises to supply what you lack. His strength is not limited by your weakness. In fact, He meets you *because* of it.

Where you feel worn down, He lifts you up. Where your energy ends, His begins. Where you are weak, He is strong, and His strength is enough for you.

Prayer:
Lord, renew my strength today. Lift the weight of my fatigue and fill me with Your power.

Call to Action:

Where do you need God to renew your strength?

_____

_____

_____

_____

_____

Day 12: The Hidden Wounds

Scripture: *The Lord is nigh unto them that are of a broken heart; and saveth such as be of a contrite spirit.*
Psalm 34:18

Some injuries leave scars the eye can trace. Others leave nothing visible at all. Yet they ache far deeper than anyone realizes. Not every wound shows up on the surface, and veterans often carry the kind that stays hidden beneath the uniform, beneath the smile, beneath the years that have passed.

Many carry wounds no one else can see: fear that follows them into quiet moments, guilt from choices made under pressure, regret over things they wish they could change, discouragement that whispers when life gets heavy, or emotional pain that lingers long after the crisis ended. Others deal with physical reminders: chronic sinus issues, sleep apnea, joint pain, injuries that never fully healed, silent proof that the body remembers battles the mind tries to forget.

But God specializes in healing the wounds no human eye can detect.

He sees the places where you feel worn down. He notices the struggles you bury under responsibility and routine. He hears the prayers you never speak out loud. He knows the battles inside your heart even when you try to minimize them.

You're not weak because you feel pain. You're not broken because you carry burdens that don't fade overnight.

You're not alone just because others don't understand what you fight through daily.

God draws especially close to the wounded, those who protect others while quietly hurting themselves, those who hide their pain well, those who learned long ago to keep marching no matter what.

He knows. He cares. And He is already at work in the places no one else can see.

Prayer:
Jesus, heal the wounds inside me, the ones no one sees. Restore my heart and remind me I am never alone.

Call to Action:

What hidden struggle do you need to bring before the Lord today?

_____

_____

_____

_____

_____

Day 13: The Veteran's Purpose

Scripture: *For we are his workmanship, created in Christ Jesus unto good works, which God hath before ordained that we should walk in them. Ephesians 2:10*

Sometimes veterans find themselves asking a quiet but honest question: *What is my purpose now?*
The mission is over. The uniform is gone. The structure that once gave clarity and direction has changed. Civilian life can feel unsteady, unfamiliar, and far different from the world you once knew so well. It's easy to wonder where you fit and what role you're meant to play now.

But your purpose didn't end when your service ended.

God didn't stop shaping your future when you took off the uniform. He didn't put your calling on a shelf. In fact, God often uses veterans in extraordinary ways because of what they've learned, discipline under pressure, compassion for others, the ability to lead, to endure, to serve, and to sacrifice. Those qualities didn't disappear. They're still in you, and God weaves them into new missions with new meaning.

Your story matters: every chapter, every struggle, every victory.
Your voice matters: your perspective, your wisdom, your testimony.

Your presence in your home, your church, and your community matters more than you realize.

God handcrafted you with intention. Your identity is not tied to a uniform or a rank but to a purpose that stretches beyond your years of military service. You still have influence. You still have gifts. You still have a mission.

The Kingdom still needs you, your strength, your compassion, your courage, and your faithfulness.

Your purpose is not in the past.
It is alive, active, and unfolding right now.

Prayer:
Father, reveal the purpose You have for me today. Use my experiences to serve and strengthen others.

Call to Action:

What is one way you can walk in your God-given purpose today?

_____

_____

_____

_____

_____

Day 14: The Shepherd Who Knows the Way

Scripture: *He maketh me to lie down in green pastures: he leadeth me beside the still waters.   Psalm 23:2*

In the military, good leadership meant everything. A leader who knew the terrain, understood the conditions, and anticipated danger could change the outcome of an entire mission. You trusted leaders who walked the ground, who studied the map, who didn't leave their people guessing. Leadership like that gave confidence, direction, and courage.

In life, Jesus becomes your Shepherd, the One who knows every valley, every detour, every obstacle, and every threat long before you encounter it. He isn't a distant commander who shouts instructions from the rear. He leads from the front. He steps into the unknown ahead of you so you don't have to fear what comes next.

He goes first. He walks ahead of you. He protects you as He guides you. He remains close enough for you to hear His voice, even in the storm.

If you feel uncertain today, about your health, your family, your work, your future, or your calling, remember this unshakable truth: you are not navigating alone. The One who leads you understands the terrain better than you ever could.

The Shepherd knows the way. He sees what's around the bend. He guards your steps with wisdom and love.
And He has never, *not once*, led you in the wrong direction.

Trust His leadership. You are in the hands of the One who knows exactly where you're going.

Prayer:
Lord, lead me today. Calm my fears and guide my steps beside Your still waters.

Call to Action:

Where do you need to follow God instead of leading yourself?

_____

_____

_____

_____

_____

Day 15: Strength in the Stillness

Scripture: *Be still, and know that I am God: I will be exalted among the heathen, I will be exalted in the earth. Psalm 46:10*

Stillness doesn't come naturally to veterans. You were trained to move, to react, to assess threats, and to make decisions quickly. Silence was rarely comforting, it often signaled that something was about to happen. Your body learned to stay alert, and your mind learned to stay active. Even now, years later, true stillness can feel unfamiliar or even unsafe.

But spiritual stillness is something entirely different.

It's not shutting down. It's not doing nothing. It's not pretending everything is fine.

Spiritual stillness is trust, deep, settled trust.

Stillness says:
"I don't have to fix everything today."
"I don't have to carry what isn't mine to carry."
"I don't have to control the outcome."
"I don't have to fear what I can't see."
"I can rest because God is God, and I am His."

Stillness is the posture of a heart that knows who's really in command.

Your strength doesn't always show in how hard you push or how much you endure. Sometimes your greatest strength

is revealed in how completely you trust the One who leads you. Rest isn't weakness. Stillness isn't laziness. It's not a lack of discipline, it's a demonstration of faith.

Stepping back, breathing deeply, and letting God hold what you cannot is a form of courage too.

Stillness is not the absence of action. It is the presence of trust.

Prayer:
God, help me find strength in stillness. Quiet my heart so I can hear Your voice.

Call to Action:

How can you create a moment of stillness with God today?

_____

_____

_____

_____

_____

Day 16: Spiritual PT

Scripture: *...exercise thyself rather unto godliness.*
1 Timothy 4:7

Physical training was non-negotiable in the military.
Whether you liked it or not, you trained. You built
endurance, strength, and resilience one rep at a time.

But spiritual strength works the same way.
You don't grow by accident.
You grow by discipline.

Prayer is PT.
Scripture is PT.
Worship is PT.
Serving is PT.
Obedience is PT.

You don't need to be perfect to grow, you just need to
show up.

Some days your spiritual PT might feel weak. That's okay.
Even on days your knees hurt, your breathing feels rough,
or your sleep apnea leaves you exhausted, your spirit can
still grow because God supplies the strength.

Spiritual fitness isn't about performance. It's about
consistency.

Prayer:
Lord, strengthen me as I train my spirit. Give me discipline to grow every day.

Call to Action:

What spiritual habit can you "train" in today?

_____

_____

_____

_____

_____

Day 17: The Veteran's Testimony

Scripture: *Let the redeemed of the Lord say so, whom he hath redeemed from the hand of the enemy.*
Psalm 107:2

Every veteran has stories, some you share, some you don't, some that come back at unexpected times. But God can redeem every part of your story, even the difficult chapters.

Your testimony is powerful.
Not because it's dramatic, but because it's real.

Maybe you've faced health struggles, chronic pain, sleepless nights, anxiety, fear, or moments of deep discouragement. But you're still here. God still carried you through. You are a living testimony of His faithfulness.

There's someone out there who needs to hear about the battles you've overcome, not to glorify your strength but to glorify God's.

Tell your story. Your testimony may be the weapon that breaks someone else's chains.

Prayer:
Father, use my story for Your glory. Help me share it with
courage and humility.

Call to Action:

Who could benefit from hearing a part of your story?

_____

_____

_____

_____

_____

Day 18: When the Past Shows Up Uninvited

Scripture: *Remember ye not the former things, neither consider the things of old.   Isaiah 43:18*

Sometimes memories hit without warning. A sound, a smell, a dream, or even a moment of stress can pull you back into scenes you believed were buried. Suddenly, emotions you thought had quieted are loud again. The past has a way of resurfacing, especially for veterans who lived through moments that most people will never fully understand.

God never asks you to deny your past or pretend those experiences didn't shape you. He doesn't expect you to erase memories or ignore the impact they've had. Instead, He invites you not to *live* in those old places. You honor your past by acknowledging it honestly, learning from it, and then allowing God to lead you forward one step at a time.

Your past shaped you, but it does not define you. Your worth is not tied to the hardest days you lived through. Your identity is not rooted in what you saw, what you carried, or what you endured.

Your identity is in Christ, secure, unchanging, and stronger than any memory that tries to pull you backward.

So when old memories rise to the surface, when the past tries to reclaim space in your present, gently remind yourself:

"I am not who I was. I am who God is making me. My story didn't end back there, God is still writing it today."

The past may knock, but it no longer owns the house.

Prayer:
Lord, heal the places where my past still echoes. Help me move forward in Your grace.

Call to Action:

What past memory do you need to surrender to God?

_____

_____

_____

_____

_____

Day 19: The Veteran's Resilience

Scripture: *We are troubled on every side, yet not distressed; we are perplexed, but not in despair; Persecuted, but not forsaken; cast down, but not destroyed."* *2 Corinthians 4:8–9*

Military training instills resilience, learning to push beyond limits, endure hardship, and stand firm under pressure. You were taught to keep moving when your body protested, to stay focused when your surroundings were chaotic, and to hold your ground when everything in you wanted to retreat. That kind of resilience carried you through some of the toughest moments of your life.

But the resilience God gives is even stronger, stronger than muscle, stronger than mindset, stronger than anything learned through training alone.

Life hits hard in ways no field manual ever explained.
Health declines or becomes unpredictable.
Responsibilities grow heavier as the years pass.
Fatigue settles into your bones.
And sometimes the spiritual battles feel relentless, striking at your peace, your confidence, or your hope.

Yet Scripture speaks a powerful promise over you:

You may be pressed, but you will not be crushed.
You may be knocked down, but you will not be destroyed.
You may feel stretched thin, but you will not fall apart.

And the reason is simple: it's not your toughness keeping you standing. It's God.

Your resilience has never been yours alone. The strength you've drawn on throughout your life, both in uniform and beyond, has been reinforced by God from the beginning. He has been the steady foundation beneath every step you managed to take, even when you didn't recognize it.

The same God who upheld you then is upholding you now. And His strength will never run out.

Prayer:
God, thank You for strengthening me when I feel worn down. Remind me that You hold me together.

Call to Action:

What is one example of God sustaining you this week?

_____

_____

_____

_____

_____

Day 20: Guarding the Gate

Scripture: *Keep thy heart with all diligence; for out of it are the issues of life. Proverbs 4:23*

In the military, guarding an entry point was a serious responsibility. You didn't wave people through casually. You verified, checked credentials, scanned for threats, and stayed alert. You understood that what you allowed in could affect everyone inside. Vigilance wasn't optional, lives depended on it.

Your heart is a gate too.

And just like a guarded post, not everything that approaches should be granted access.

Negative voices that tear you down.
Harmful influences that pull you off course.
Unhealthy habits that slowly drain your strength.
Discouraging thoughts that speak defeat.
Old temptations that try to slip back in unnoticed.

All of these seek entry.

God calls you to guard your heart, not with fear or suspicion, but with wisdom and discernment. You are the gatekeeper of your own inner life. You decide what gets close to your spirit, what shapes your mindset, and what earns a place in your thoughts.

Just because something knocks doesn't mean you open the door.
Just because a thought arrives doesn't mean you entertain it.

Just because a temptation feels familiar doesn't mean you welcome it inside.

Stand post at your heart today.

Let truth pass through.
Let encouragement and godly influence enter freely.
Keep lies, negativity, and old patterns outside the wire where they belong.

Your heart is worth guarding.
And with God's help, you can protect what He has entrusted to you.

Prayer:
Lord, help me guard my heart with wisdom and strength.
Show me what to let in and what to keep out.

Call to Action:

What negative voice or influence do you need to shut out today?

_____

_____

_____

_____

_____

Day 21: When God Says "Rest"

Scripture: *He maketh me to lie down in green pastures: he leadeth me beside the still waters.   Psalm 23:2*

Rest is hard for veterans. Stillness can feel uncomfortable. Sleep doesn't always come easily. Even when the body slows down, the mind keeps moving.

But God sometimes *makes* you rest. Not as punishment, but as protection.

When your body is worn down from years of strain…
When your sinuses flare and you can't breathe right…
When fatigue hits from sleep apnea…
When your joints ache…

God whispers:
"Rest. Let Me restore you."

Rest isn't something you earn.
It's something God grants.

And when you rest in Him, He rebuilds what life has worn down.

Prayer:
Father, teach me to rest in You. Restore what exhaustion has taken from me.

Call to Action:

What is one way you can intentionally rest today?

_____

_____

_____

_____

_____

Day 22: The Desert Seasons

Scripture: *Behold, I will do a new thing; now it shall spring forth; shall ye not know it? I will even make a way in the wilderness, and rivers in the desert. Isaiah 43:19*

Many veterans know what it's like to operate in harsh environments: deserts, jungles, etc,, places that challenged the body, tested mental endurance, and pushed every limit you had. Heat, cold, exhaustion, isolation, long stretches of waiting, or moments of intense uncertainty. Those experiences leave a mark. They shape how you understand difficulty and how you endure it.

Life has its own version of deserts too.

There are days when prayer feels dry and you're not sure what to say. Days when Scripture feels distant, even though you're trying to stay connected. Days when your spirit feels empty or worn thin. Days when God seems quiet, and you wonder if He's still near.

These spiritual deserts can feel as draining as any physical hardship you've faced. They are seasons where strength feels limited and clarity seems far away.

But God works in desert places more often than we realize. Throughout Scripture, He meets people in their wilderness seasons, bringing renewal where exhaustion once lived, offering direction where confusion settled, and providing comfort when hearts felt worn down. God has a way of restoring what feels dry and strengthening what feels weak.

Your desert season is not without purpose. Even when it feels quiet or difficult, God is present. He is preparing your

heart, shaping your faith, and laying groundwork for what comes next. What feels barren now may become the place where you grow in ways you never expected.

You are not forgotten in the desert. God is already doing something new.

Prayer:
Lord, meet me in my desert seasons. Bring refreshment to the dry places of my soul.

Call to Action:

What dry area of your life needs God's refreshing?

_____

_____

_____

_____

_____

Day 23: The Unseen Battle

Scripture: *For we wrestle not against flesh and blood, but against principalities, against powers, against the rulers of the darkness of this world, against spiritual wickedness in high places. Ephesians 6:12*

Veterans understand the reality of unseen enemies. You learned early on to respect threats that didn't announce themselves, dangers that hid in shadows, movements you couldn't quite identify, and conflicts where the line between safety and risk was invisible. That awareness shaped how you approached every mission.

Spiritually, the challenges you face now share that same hidden nature. The struggles aren't always physical or visible. They show up in moments of uncertainty, in thoughts that pull you off course, in temptations that seem harmless at first, in discouragement that settles in quietly, or in fear and anxiety that rise without warning. These battles don't appear on a radar screen, yet they can feel just as real and just as draining as anything you once faced.

The hope you hold onto is that you never face these struggles by yourself. God equips you with what you need for the challenges ahead, and Christ gives you strength when you feel worn down or overwhelmed. The Holy Spirit offers guidance in moments when you're unsure of your next step, and God's presence surrounds you even when the conflict is invisible.

So stay watchful, but don't let fear take over. The same God who stood with you in every visible battle stands with you in the unseen ones as well. His protection is steady, His

strength is reliable, and His presence is constant, even when the fight is hard to define.

Prayer:
Lord, help me recognize the real battles I face today. Strengthen me to fight with faith.

Call to Action:

Where do you sense spiritual warfare happening right now?

_____

_____

_____

_____

_____

Day 24: Marching by Faith

Scripture: *We walk by faith, not by sight.*
2 Corinthians 5:7

You marched through conditions where visibility was low and certainty was thin. There were moments when the terrain was unclear, when the weather worked against you, or when the situation shifted faster than you could process. Yet you kept moving because you trusted your training, the people leading you, and the team beside you. That trust helped you step forward even when your eyes couldn't tell you what was coming next.

Faith works much the same way. Walking with God often means moving forward when sight fails, continuing the journey when answers seem delayed, when prayers don't appear to be answered in the way you hoped, or when the path ahead feels confusing or unfinished. These moments test the heart in ways no physical challenge ever could.

But faith doesn't demand flawless certainty. It doesn't require you to feel strong every day or to have every step figured out. Faith grows from a willingness to take the next step, even if it feels small, even if you wish the road were clearer. God sees the terrain long before you reach it. He knows the dangers you can't detect, the turns you don't anticipate, and the challenges you don't yet see. His guidance is precise, steady, and reliable.

So move forward today, not because you see everything clearly, but because you trust the One who does. Walking by faith means placing your confidence in God's vision rather than your own.

Take the next step.
Let Him lead.
He will not guide you wrong.

Prayer:
Lord, help me walk by faith. Guide my steps even when I
cannot see the way.

Call to Action:

What step of faith can you take without seeing the whole path?

_____

_____

_____

_____

_____

Day 25: The Veteran's Strength

Scripture: *...for the joy of the Lord is your strength.*
Nehemiah 8:10

Strength meant something different in the military. It was physical, measurable, and often proven through endurance, performance, or the ability to push past pain. Strength was something you could see, test, and demonstrate. It had weight and muscle behind it.

But the strength God offers reaches far deeper than anything the body can produce. Scripture describes this strength as joy, something quiet, steady, and rooted in who God is rather than in how capable you feel on a given day.

Joy is not naïve optimism, and it isn't pretending everything is fine. It doesn't ignore hardship or minimize real struggles. Instead, joy is the deep assurance that God is good, present, and faithful even when life is difficult. It's the inner steadiness that holds you when circumstances shift or when your own strength feels limited.

You may notice changes in your body now, tiredness that shows up more often, joints that ache from years of wear, nights of disrupted sleep, or energy that doesn't come as easily as it used to. These realities are part of life, and they can weigh on the heart as much as the body.

Yet even in seasons of physical strain or emotional fatigue, God's joy remains a source of spiritual strength. It lifts you when you feel worn down. It restores what the world drains. It reminds you that your foundation is secure, not

because of how strong you feel, but because of how faithful God is.

Choose joy today, not as a way to deny struggle, but as a way to anchor your heart in God's goodness. His joy is strength that doesn't fade with time, injury, or age. It is strength that holds.

Prayer:
Father, fill me with Your joy today. Strengthen my spirit beyond what my body can do.

Call to Action:

What blessing can you thank God for right now?

_____

_____

_____

_____

_____

Day 26: Enemy Lies

Scripture: *And ye shall know the truth, and the truth shall make you free. John 8:32*

The enemy rarely shouts. He speaks in whispers, subtle thoughts that slide into your mind during quiet moments, often sounding like your own voice. Those whispers say things like, *"You're not enough... You've failed too much... You should be stronger... You're alone... God must be disappointed in you."* They hit hard because they aim at old wounds, past experiences, and places where you already feel vulnerable. Lies gain power when they echo something you fear might be true.

But truth always exposes lies.

And God's truth tells a very different story. It reminds you that you are forgiven, completely and without conditions. It declares that you are chosen with purpose and loved without hesitation. It assures you that you are never walking through life alone, no matter how isolated you may feel in the moment. And it reveals that God takes joy in you as His child. Not reluctantly, not barely, but genuinely.

The most powerful weapon against lies is Scripture. God's Word anchors you when emotions shift and reminds you who you really are when the enemy tries to pull you backward. When you speak Scripture, pray it, and stand firmly on it, the whispers lose their strength. Little by little, truth replaces deception, confidence replaces fear, and the chains that once felt unbreakable begin to fall.

Fill your mind with God's promises. Let His voice become louder than any whisper meant to harm you. Truth doesn't just challenge lies, it breaks them.

Prayer:
Lord, expose every lie the enemy has spoken over me. Fill me with Your truth.

Call to Action:

What lie do you need to replace with God's truth?

_____

_____

_____

_____

_____

Day 27: The Veteran's Calling

Scripture: *A man's gift maketh room for him, and bringeth him before great men.   Proverbs 18:16*

Veterans often struggle to recognize their gifts once the uniform is gone. The structure, identity, and sense of mission that came with service can make it easy to overlook the strengths that were part of you long before you ever stepped into the military. Yet God placed those abilities within you from the beginning, leadership that rises in difficult moments, courage that shows itself under pressure, problem-solving instincts, initiative when others hesitate, and a deep sense of faithfulness and responsibility.

Your time in service shaped those qualities, but it didn't create them. And they didn't disappear when your military chapter ended. You may no longer wear the rank or the uniform, but you are still part of a greater mission. You are a soldier in the Kingdom of God, and the calling He has placed on your life continues into every season that follows.

Your purpose isn't something left behind in the past. It stands before you right now. Woven into your family life, your church involvement, your ministry opportunities, your workplace, and your community. Everywhere you go, God is able to use your experience, your resilience, and your perspective in ways that many people around you simply cannot offer.

Veterans bring insights and strengths that are shaped by real sacrifice and lived experience. Your voice carries weight. Your story offers hope. Your presence brings

stability and encouragement to people who might be walking through their own quiet battles.

Lean into the calling God has placed on your life. The gifts He gave you still matter, still have purpose, and are still being used for something meaningful.

God is not finished with you.
Not even close.

Prayer:
Lord, reveal and activate the calling You've placed in me. Use me for Your glory.

Call to Action:

What gift or ability can you use today for God's glory?

_____

_____

_____

_____

_____

Day 28: Healing Takes Time

Scripture: *He healeth the broken in heart, and bindeth up their wounds. Psalm 147:3*

Healing isn't instant, physically or spiritually. Your body has endured years of strain, injury, and wear. Your spirit has carried burdens that few people fully understand. Some wounds fade quickly, while others take time, attention, and grace. Healing rarely happens all at once. More often, it unfolds slowly, layer by layer.

Healing is a process.
A journey.
A steady walk rather than a sprint.

It is a cooperation between God's restoring touch and your willingness to let Him do the work. Sometimes that means resting when you'd rather push forward. Sometimes it means acknowledging old hurts you'd prefer to ignore. And sometimes it means allowing God to speak truth into places where pain has lived for far too long.

When progress feels slow, don't let discouragement take over. Slow healing is still healing. Even the scars you carry, physical, emotional, or spiritual, are not signs of defeat. They testify to survival, resilience, and the ways God has carried you through seasons you didn't think you'd make it through.

God is patient with you, far more patient than you often are with yourself. He never rushes your growth, never shames your pace, and never compares your journey to someone else's. He walks with you step by step, giving strength for today and hope for tomorrow.

So extend that same patience toward yourself.
Healing is happening, even on the days you can't feel it.
And God will finish the work He has begun in you.

Prayer:
Father, continue healing my wounds. Give me grace for the
slow parts of my journey.

Call to Action:

What area of your life requires patience while God heals?

_____

_____

_____

_____

_____

Day 29: Your Family as Your Mission Field

Scripture: *...but as for me and my house, we will serve the Lord. Joshua 24:15*

In the military, the mission always came first. Decisions were shaped by purpose, responsibility, and the understanding that what you did mattered to the people beside you. After service, the mission looks different, but it is no less important. Your mission field shifts from a structured environment to the place where your life unfolds. Your home.

Your family becomes the people entrusted to your care. Your spouse, your children, your grandchildren, and even future generations you may never meet are influenced by the choices you make today. The way you speak, the example you set, the way you show love, and the prayers you whisper over your family create a foundation that lasts far beyond your lifetime.

You are a covering for the people you love. A source of protection, stability, and spiritual guidance. The habits you cultivate, the faith you demonstrate, and the integrity you live out have a quiet but powerful ripple effect. What you model in your home shapes the atmosphere your family grows in and the legacy they will carry forward.

Every day, your home becomes a place where Christ is honored simply because you choose to lead with humility, patience, and love. You may not always feel like you're doing enough, but your presence, your prayers, and your faithfulness matter more than you realize.

Your family is not only part of your life, it is one of your greatest ministries. God has placed you there with purpose, and He will give you everything you need to lead well.

Prayer:
Lord, help me lead my family in faith. Strengthen my home and guide me as I guide them.

Call to Action:

How can you serve or encourage your family today?

_____

_____

_____

_____

_____

Day 30: God's Presence in the Quiet

Scripture: *For thus saith the Lord God, the Holy One of Israel; In returning and rest shall ye be saved; in quietness and in confidence shall be your strength... Isaiah 30:15*

Veterans often struggle with quiet moments. After years of constant activity, structure, noise, and alertness, silence can feel foreign, even unsettling. When things grow still, the mind has space to wander, and that space sometimes fills with memories, worries, or thoughts you didn't ask for. It's easy to feel like quiet is something to avoid rather than embrace.

But God often meets His people in the quiet.
Not in the chaos of a crowded day.
Not in the constant noise of responsibilities.
Not in the distractions that pull your attention in every direction.

Quietness is where His voice becomes clearer, where His presence feels closer, and where your spirit finally has room to breathe.

Take a moment today, just a few minutes, to slow your pace. Set aside the pressure to perform or accomplish something. Sit with God without an agenda, without needing the moment to be perfect, and without trying to force anything spiritual to happen. Simply breathe and be present with Him.

Stillness is not emptiness. It isn't wasted time. It is space God uses to renew your heart, untangle your thoughts, and speak life into places that have grown weary.

In the quiet, God restores what the noise has worn down.

Prayer:
Lord, meet me in the quiet. Strengthen me through trust in Your presence.

Call to Action:

When will you set aside a quiet moment for God today?

_____

_____

_____

_____

_____

Day 31: When You Feel Outnumbered

Scripture: *What shall we then say to these things? If God be for us, who can be against us?   Romans 8:31*

There were moments in the military when the odds didn't look great. Too many unknowns. Too few reassurances. But a well-trained soldier learns to stand firm even when outnumbered.

Spiritually, you will face days that feel overwhelming, illness, stress, financial burdens, responsibilities, or pressure that outmatches your strength. You may feel surrounded by problems with no support in sight.

But the truth is this: You are never outnumbered.
Not with God beside you.
Not with His angels surrounding you.
Not with His Spirit within you.

Even when the world stacks against you, heaven stacks in your favor.

Stand firm today.
Victory is not determined by numbers, it's determined by Who fights for you.

Prayer:
Lord, remind me that with You on my side, I will never be outnumbered.

Call to Action:

What fear or problem do you need to place under God's authority?

_____

_____

_____

_____

_____

Day 32: The Veteran's Leadership

Scripture: *...whosoever will be great among you, let him be your minister.   Matthew 20:26*

You learned leadership through action, not through titles or long speeches. The leaders you respected most were never the loud ones. They were the ones who showed up consistently, made sacrifices quietly, and carried themselves with steady confidence. They earned trust because they cared for their people, paid attention, and led from the front when it mattered. Those examples shaped the way you see leadership even now.

Jesus teaches leadership in that same spirit. His model is not built on force, pressure, or demanding authority, but on service. He leads by lowering Himself, by lifting others, and by giving more than He receives. When you look at the way He served, you can see reflections of the kind of leadership you witnessed in your own time of service.

Your years in uniform prepared you to lead your family, your church, and your community with that same mix of humility and strength. You lead not by pushing people forward, but by being someone worth following. You lead when you choose to serve without recognition, when you love even on the days you feel worn down, and when you keep showing up simply because faithfulness matters. Your willingness to prioritize others over yourself quietly shapes the people around you and creates a legacy that reaches further than you know.

This is what Kingdom leadership looks like. It is what Christ-like leadership feels like. And in a world hungry for steady, compassionate, trustworthy examples, the way you lead, humbly, faithfully, and with a servant's heart, is a gift the world deeply needs.

Prayer:
Lord, mold me into a servant leader. Help me guide others with humility and love.

Call to Action:

Where can you lead by serving today?

_____

_____

_____

_____

_____

Day 33: The Battle Within

Scripture: *Watch and pray, that ye enter not into temptation: the spirit indeed is willing, but the flesh is weak. Matthew 26:41*

Some battles come from the outside, pressing in through circumstances, responsibilities, or the demands of daily life. But some of the hardest battles are the ones fought within, the quiet struggles happening in the mind, the body, and the heart. You know exactly what it feels like when your spirit is willing and eager to move forward, yet your body seems determined to slow you down. There are days when sinus issues flare without warning, when sleep apnea robs you of the rest you desperately need, when pain creeps into your joints and makes every movement feel heavier, and when anxiety rises up and drains your strength before the day even begins.

Jesus often pointed out that spiritual battles don't usually start with what we can see on the outside. They begin deep within us, where our intentions, fears, hopes, wounds, and faith collide. You may have every desire to do what is right, to push on, to trust God fully, yet still feel limited by a body that doesn't always cooperate or a mind that struggles to quiet itself. It's easy to mistake those moments for weakness or failure, but they aren't. They are reminders that being human comes with limitations, and those limitations are not the end of the story.

Weakness is not defeat. It is an honest place where you become aware of how much you need God's strength to carry what you cannot. When your body falters, when fatigue rises, when anxiety tightens its grip, that is the very place where God invites you to lean more fully on Him. His

strength does not depend on yours. His power is not diminished by your tiredness. And His presence is most often felt in the moments when you realize you can't move forward on your own.

When your body resists and your spirit feels stretched thin, turn your weight toward Him. Let His strength fill the gap. Let His grace steady your steps. And let His presence remind you that even in your internal battles, you are never fighting alone.

Prayer:
Father, strengthen my spirit when my body feels weak. Fight the battles inside me with Your power.

Call to Action:

What internal struggle do you need to bring to God?

_____

_____

_____

_____

_____

Day 34: Holding the High Ground

Scripture: *The name of the Lord is a strong tower: the righteous runneth into it, and is safe.* *Proverbs 18:10*

In every conflict, anyone who has spent time studying strategy knows how important the high ground is. It offers a clearer view of what's ahead, a stronger defensive position, and the ability to respond with confidence rather than fear. The one who holds the high ground has the advantage, because they aren't overwhelmed by what they can't see. They stand where the landscape makes sense and where danger is easier to recognize and prepare for.

In your life, God Himself is that high ground. He is the place where perspective becomes clearer and where your footing becomes steady. When storms begin to build around you and uncertainty starts closing in, your safest move is always upward, toward Him. When threats or anxieties crowd close, you can take refuge in His presence, knowing His name is a shield stronger than anything trying to push against you. And when fear tries to rise up inside you, you don't have to stand on the same level as your enemy. You can stand higher, anchored in the One who sees the full picture.

You're not fighting your battles from a valley where everything feels overwhelming and out of control. You're fighting them from a fortified position, held, strengthened, and guarded by the God who has never lost a battle. His strength surrounds you, His authority covers you, and His protection gives you the advantage you would never have on your own.

So run to Him today. Hold tightly to the high ground He provides. From there, you can face every challenge with courage, because you're standing with the One who lifts you above the shadows and keeps your footing firm.

Prayer:
Lord, be my strong tower. Lift me above the battles that threaten my peace.

Call to Action:

Where do you need to take spiritual refuge today?

_____

_____

_____

_____

_____

Day 35: The Power of a Clean Slate

Scripture: *Come now, and let us reason together, saith the Lord: though your sins be as scarlet, they shall be as white as snow; though they be red like crimson, they shall be as wool. Isaiah 1:18*

In basic training, one of the greatest gifts you were given was the chance to start over. It didn't matter what you had been before you arrived, your habits, your mistakes, your reputation, or the choices you regretted. The moment you stepped onto that training field, you were handed a clean slate. New expectations were set, new standards were taught, and a new identity began to form. You were being shaped into someone with purpose, discipline, and direction, and the weight of who you once were no longer held authority over who you were becoming.

God offers that same kind of clean slate, not just once, but every single day. No matter what has happened in your past, no matter where you've stumbled, no matter how long you've been fighting the same battles or carrying the same regrets, His forgiveness remains complete. It isn't partial or conditional. It doesn't fade with time or depend on how well you performed this week. In Christ, you are forgiven entirely, washed clean, made new, and released from the burdens you once carried.

Because of that, your past no longer has the right to dictate who you are today. The mistakes that once haunted you do not get to determine your future or limit what God can do through your life. You are not defined by your failures; you are defined by the grace that covers them.

So walk today with the confidence of someone who has truly been set free. Stand tall in the identity God has given you, knowing that every day is a fresh start with new strength, new mercy, and new purpose.

Prayer:
Jesus, thank You for wiping my slate clean. Help me live in the freedom You purchased for me.

Call to Action:

What guilt or regret do you need to release?

_____

_____

_____

_____

_____

Day 36: The Value of Discipline

Scripture: *Now no chastening for the present seemeth to be joyous, but grievous: nevertheless afterward it yieldeth the peaceable fruit of righteousness unto them which are exercised thereby. Hebrews 12:11*

Discipline is woven into a veteran's life from the very beginning. You learned how to show up whether you felt ready or not, how to push past discomfort, how to endure pain, and how to remain consistent even on the days when motivation was nowhere to be found. Over time, that discipline became part of who you were. It shaped your habits, your mindset, and the way you approached every challenge placed in front of you.

God develops spiritual discipline in much the same way. He guides you through His Word, teaching you step by step. He brings correction not to shame you, but to steer you toward what is good and life-giving. He allows you to walk through difficult seasons that test your resolve, yet those seasons also strengthen your faith in ways comfort never could. What He does in your spiritual life mirrors what you experienced in uniform: steady growth that comes from trusting the process and refusing to quit.

Spiritual discipline is not punishment. It is preparation, God shaping your character, sharpening your focus, and building endurance in your heart. Every difficult moment you push through leaves something valuable behind. It produces righteousness as you learn to choose what is right, peace as you learn to trust Him more fully, maturity as you

grow beyond old patterns, and strength that carries you into the next season.

God isn't trying to break you down or wear you out. He is forming something strong, steady, and resilient in you. He is building a warrior of faith, one patient step at a time.

Prayer:
Lord, help me receive Your discipline with humility. Shape me into the man You've called me to be.

Call to Action:

What spiritual discipline can you practice today?

_____

_____

_____

_____

_____

Day 37: When Directions Don't Make Sense

Scripture: *Thy word is a lamp unto my feet, and a light unto my path.   Psalm 119:105*

In the military, you didn't always need the whole plan, just your part. You followed orders even when you didn't understand the bigger picture.

God leads the same way.
He gives enough light for the next step, not the entire journey.

Sometimes you want clarity about the future,
What's next?
Where am I supposed to go?
How will this problem be solved?
What is God doing in my life?

But Scripture says His Word is a lamp for your *feet*, not a floodlight for the whole road.

One step at a time.
One instruction at a time.
One day at a time.

Trust the next step God has already lit for you.

Prayer:
God, guide my next step. Help me trust Your leading even when I don't see the full plan.

Call to Action:

What next step do you sense God asking of you?

_____

_____

_____

_____

_____

Day 38: The Veteran's Prayer Life

Scripture: *Pray without ceasing.   1 Thessalonians 5:17*

Prayer doesn't have to be complicated or formal. As a veteran, you learned the value of being direct, honest, and straightforward, and that's exactly the kind of communication God invites from you. He's not looking for perfect wording or carefully crafted speeches. He welcomes you just as you are, with your real thoughts, real struggles, and real needs.

Prayer isn't a ceremony reserved for special moments or sacred spaces. It's a conversation, a steady line of communication between you and the God who walks with you. You can pray while you're driving down the road, while you're working with your hands, while you're facing a decision that feels heavy, or when you're simply exhausted and trying to make it through the day. You can pray when frustration rises, when joy surprises you, when memories weigh on your mind, or when peace finally settles in.

Your prayer life doesn't need polish; it needs presence. God isn't moved by how long your words are, how eloquent they sound, or how impressive they might seem to someone else. What moves Him is the sincerity behind them, the honest heart that reaches toward Him in both strength and weakness.

Keep that line of communication open. Let prayer become a natural part of your rhythm, woven into the moments of

your day. Talk to Him often, freely, and without hesitation, knowing He hears you every time.

Prayer:
Lord, keep me talking with You. Help me build a constant connection with Your presence.

Call to Action:

What short prayer can you pray every hour today?

_____

_____

_____

_____

_____

Day 39: A Heart for Service

Scripture: *...but by love serve one another.*
Galatians 5:13

Service became part of who you were from the moment
you put on the uniform. It wasn't something you had to
learn; it was something you lived. You stepped forward
when your country needed you, stood between danger and
those who couldn't defend themselves, and carried
responsibilities that required courage, sacrifice, and a
willingness to put others first. That instinct, to serve, to
protect, to stand in the gap, became woven into your
identity.

Now God invites you to bring that same heart into His
Kingdom. The places you serve may look different, but the
purpose is just as meaningful. You serve when you invest
in your church and help strengthen the body of believers.
You serve when you show up for your community and
offer support in ways others might overlook. You serve
when you give time, attention, and love to your family,
building a foundation of faith that will shape generations.
You serve when you encourage someone who is hurting or
walk beside someone who feels alone. In all these
moments, your willingness to step forward reflects the
same spirit you carried in uniform.

Service in God's Kingdom has never been about
recognition or applause. It has always been about
obedience, responding to God's call with a willing heart
and allowing Him to use your life to bless others. Your
military service had an end date, a moment when the
uniform came off and the mission shifted. But your service
to God does not end; it becomes a lifelong calling. Every

day offers another opportunity to serve with purpose, compassion, and faith, carrying out a mission far greater than anything this world can measure.

Prayer:
Jesus, strengthen my heart to serve. Help me bless others with humility and love.

Call to Action:

Who can you serve today with humility?

_____

_____

_____

_____

_____

Day 40: The Value of Your Voice

Scripture: *Wherefore comfort yourselves together, and edify one another, even as also ye do.*
1 Thessalonians 5:11

Veterans often underestimate the impact their words can have. You've lived through hardship, pressure, and seasons that tested you in ways many people will never fully understand. Because of that, when you offer encouragement, it carries a weight and credibility that others instinctively recognize. Your voice comes from experience, from resilience, and from a place of hard-earned wisdom, and that makes what you say far more powerful than you might realize.

When you speak life into someone, whether it's a child who looks up to you, a spouse who needs reassurance, a fellow believer trying to stay faithful, a friend who feels worn down, or another veteran carrying quiet burdens your heart understands, your words matter in ways you may never see. You never know when a single sentence, a moment of kindness, or a gentle reminder from you is exactly what someone has been praying for. God often places the right words on your heart at the right time, and your willingness to share them can change the direction of someone's day, or even their life.

Your voice has the power to lift someone who feels defeated and help them stand again. It can bring clarity in moments of confusion, restore hope where discouragement has settled in, and strengthen faith in someone who feels it

slipping. What you say carries influence because it comes from a place of authenticity and lived truth.

So don't hold back the encouragement God prompts you to give. Use your voice today. Someone around you needs the strength it carries.

Prayer:
Lord, help me speak encouragement today. Use my words to build others up.

Call to Action:

Who needs encouragement from you today?

_____

_____

_____

_____

_____

Day 41: When You Need Backup

Scripture: *Two are better than one; because they have a good reward for their labour. For if they fall, the one will lift up his fellow... Ecclesiastes 4:9–10*

You never went into danger alone. From the earliest days of your training, you learned the importance of having a battle buddy, someone who watched your back, helped carry the load, and stood shoulder to shoulder with you no matter what the day brought. You shared responsibilities, challenges, victories, setbacks, and the unspoken understanding that survival and success depended on sticking together. That bond wasn't optional; it was essential.

God designed life to work the exact same way. He never intended for you to face the weight of your struggles on your own. Needing people doesn't make you weak; it reveals that you were created for connection, support, and shared strength. Community isn't a sign of dependence, it's a reflection of God's design for His people to walk together, encourage one another, and lift each other up.

There will be days when you feel overwhelmed, moments when the pressure grows heavy, and seasons when the path forward seems unclear. In those times, asking for help isn't a failure, it's wisdom. Reaching out allows others to step into your life the way you once stepped into theirs. Let trusted people stand with you in the battles you face today, offering perspective, prayer, and presence.

You were never meant to fight alone. God surrounds you with people who can walk with you, just as you once walked with those who depended on you. Embrace that support, and let community become part of your strength.

Prayer:
Lord, place the right people in my life. Give me courage to reach out when I need support.

Call to Action:

Who can you ask for help or prayer today?

_____

_____

_____

_____

_____

Day 42: The Power of Obedience

Scripture: *...blessed are they that hear the word of God, and keep it. Luke 11:28*

A military member's strength has never been found only in skill or physical ability. Training matters, endurance matters, and experience matters, but obedience is what makes a soldier effective. You learned to move the moment a command was given, to stop when the situation demanded it, and to adjust your course without hesitation when orders changed. That willingness to respond quickly and trust the leadership placed over you became one of the greatest strengths you carried during your service.

Spiritually, obedience functions much the same way. It isn't something you do to earn God's approval; His love for you is already complete and unshakable. Instead, obedience positions your heart to receive what He desires to give. It opens the door for His guidance, His provision, and His power to move freely in your life. When He prompts you to forgive someone, responding with obedience softens your heart and restores peace. When He nudges you to step into an act of service, your willingness becomes a blessing not only to others but also to your own soul. When He calls you to trust Him in uncertainty, obedience becomes an act of faith that strengthens your relationship with Him. And when He reminds you to pray, stopping to talk with Him draws you into deeper closeness and clarity.

Obedience is not a burden meant to weigh you down. It's a pathway to freedom, a way of living that removes unnecessary struggles, brings alignment with God's

purpose, and allows your life to flow in step with His direction. Just as your obedience in the military brought order and strength, your obedience to God brings blessing and spiritual freedom.

Prayer:
Father, help me obey Your voice quickly and joyfully. Make me sensitive to Your direction.

Call to Action:

Where is God calling you to obey Him right now?

_____

_____

_____

_____

_____

Day 43: Standing Firm Under Pressure

Scripture: *Therefore, my beloved brethren, be ye stedfast, unmoveable, always abounding in the work of the Lord...*
1 Corinthians 15:58

Pressure reveals character.
You saw it in training.
You saw it in deployment.
And you see it now in daily life.

Life applies pressure in many forms:
health struggles
financial strain
family challenges
unexpected setbacks

But pressure doesn't break a man rooted in Christ.
It strengthens him.

Stand firm today.
Hold your ground.
God is reinforcing you in ways you cannot see.

Your endurance is preaching a sermon to those watching your life.

Prayer:
Lord, help me stay steadfast under pressure. Strengthen me to stand firm in Your truth.

Call to Action:

What truth will you cling to when pressure rises?

_____

_____

_____

_____

_____

Day 44: Listening for the Commander's Voice

Scripture: *My sheep hear my voice, and I know them, and they follow me.* John 10:27

In the chaos of training or combat, you learned something invaluable: how to recognize your leader's voice above all the noise. Even when visibility was low or confusion was high, you could still pick out the tone of authority, direction, and confidence. You didn't always have a clear view of who was giving the order, but you knew the sound well enough to act without hesitation. That ability kept you focused, steady, and safe.

God speaks to you in a similar way. He communicates through the truth of Scripture, through the gentle prompting of the Holy Spirit, through the wisdom of people He places in your life, and through the deep, steady peace that settles in your spirit when you're walking in the right direction. His voice is never confusing or condemning; it is guiding, strengthening, and full of purpose.

But just like in the field, there are always competing voices that try to drown Him out. Fear whispers worst-case scenarios. Doubt questions your worth and your calling. Anger pushes you toward impulsive reactions. Regret keeps you stuck in yesterday's failures. Distractions pull your attention away from what matters most. These voices aren't just loud, they're persistent. And if left unchecked, they can make it difficult to recognize the One voice that leads you toward life instead of confusion.

The more time you spend in God's presence, the more familiar His voice becomes. As you learn to quiet the inner noise and pause long enough to listen, His guidance grows clearer, His direction steadier, and His peace stronger. You begin to recognize His voice the way a soldier recognizes the command that cuts through chaos.

Follow His voice today. He will never lead you into danger without purpose, and He will never guide you toward anything that harms your soul. His voice always leads toward hope, strength, and the next step in His plan for your life.

Prayer:
Jesus, speak clearly to me. Help me recognize Your voice above all others.

Call to Action:

What distraction do you need to quiet to hear God more clearly?

_____

_____

_____

_____

_____

Day 45: Carried, Not Forsaken

Scripture: *And even to your old age I am he; and even to hoar hairs will I carry you… Isaiah 46:4*

There's a deep comfort in knowing God doesn't retire from caring for you. He doesn't step back as you grow older or face new challenges with your health, strength, or energy.

He promises, not just to stay with you,
but to carry you.
To sustain you.
To rescue you when you cannot carry yourself.

Your service may be behind you,
but God's service to you continues daily.

Even when your body slows,
even when fatigue hits,
even when pain lingers,
even when the future feels uncertain,
God carries you with unbreakable strength.

You are never abandoned.
Never forgotten.
Never alone.

Prayer:
Lord, thank You for carrying me through every season.
Sustain me today with Your faithful love.

Call to Action:

What burden will you let God carry today?

_____

_____

_____

_____

_____

Day 46: The Watchful Warrior

Scripture: *Watch and pray, that ye enter not into temptation: the spirit indeed is willing, but the flesh is weak.   Matthew 26:41*

Veterans are trained observers. You learned to scan for danger, anticipate threats, and stay alert in ways that never fully leave you.

Spiritually, Jesus gives the same instruction:

Watch and pray.
Not just watch.
Not just pray.
Both.

Watching keeps you alert.
Praying keeps you protected.

Your spiritual battles are won not through panic, but through awareness and communion with God. When you stay spiritually alert, you see temptation coming before it hits. You sense discouragement before it overwhelms. You recognize lies before they take root.

Keep watch today.
Pray with the vigilance of a warrior.

Prayer:
Lord, help me stay spiritually aware. Strengthen my guard and deepen my prayer life.

Call to Action:

Where do you need to stay spiritually alert?

_____

_____

_____

_____

_____

Day 47: God in the Everyday

Scripture: *In all thy ways acknowledge him, and he shall direct thy paths.   Proverbs 3:6*

God is not limited to Sunday mornings or the moments when life feels overwhelming. He is present in the ordinary, the routine, and the seemingly insignificant parts of your day. He is with you during the quiet ride to work, in the simple walk across a parking lot, in the moments you share with your kids, and even in the chores that feel repetitive or unimportant. He is there in the small pauses between distractions, those few seconds where your mind has room to breathe. Nothing is too ordinary for His presence, and nothing in your daily rhythm falls outside His care.

Veterans understand better than most how important the everyday moments truly are. Small habits, repeated consistently, often determine the success of the mission. Routine builds discipline, discipline builds strength, and strength carries you through the hardest challenges. In the same way, recognizing God in the small, quiet pieces of your life shapes your heart to follow Him when the bigger, heavier decisions come. It's in the daily awareness of His presence that your spiritual footing becomes steady.

Speaking His name throughout your day and inviting Him into even the simplest moments helps your heart stay aligned with His leading. As you walk through each task, conversation, or responsibility with an awareness of Him beside you, you'll find that He quietly straightens your path, gives clarity where there was none, and strengthens you for what lies ahead.

Prayer:
Father, help me see You in every part of my day. Guide my steps as I acknowledge You.

Call to Action:

Where can you acknowledge God in your day today?

_____

_____

_____

_____

_____

Day 48: Responding Under Pressure

Scripture: *Therefore whosoever heareth these sayings of mine, and doeth them, I will liken him unto a wise man, which built his house upon a rock.   Matthew 7:24*

Training prepares you for the moments when everything is on the line. Under pressure, you don't magically rise to some new level of ability, you fall back on whatever has been built into you through repetition, discipline, and practice. Your responses in the hardest moments come from the preparation you've already done, not from raw emotion or last-minute strength. That principle shaped your military experience, and it carries into your spiritual life just as clearly.

When spiritual pressure hits, when fear creeps in, when life becomes unpredictable, when stress weighs heavy, you don't rely on your feelings to carry you through. Feelings shift quickly, but what has been planted in your heart remains steady. Your strength comes from the truth of God's Word, the promises Christ has spoken over your life, the habits of prayer you have cultivated, and the discipline of obedience you have learned over time. These practices form a spiritual foundation that doesn't disappear the moment a storm arrives.

Jesus never hid the fact that storms will come. He made it clear that every person, no matter how strong or faithful, will face seasons that test their endurance. But the storm is never a sign of weakness. It doesn't expose your flaws, it reveals your foundation. And if your foundation is Christ, then even when everything around you shakes, you remain

standing. You may feel the wind and the weight of the moment, but you will not collapse, because your strength comes from a source deeper and stronger than anything you face.

With Christ beneath you and within you, no storm has the power to take you down.

Prayer:
Lord, strengthen my foundation. Help me respond under pressure with faith instead of fear.

Call to Action:

How can you respond in faith instead of emotion?

_____

_____

_____

_____

_____

Day 49: Military Bearing, Spiritual Bearing

Scripture: *Let your moderation be known unto all men. The Lord is at hand.   Philippians 4:5*

In uniform, you learned the importance of bearing, the way you carried yourself, the steadiness you maintained under pressure, and the discipline you showed even when eyes were on you and expectations were high. Bearing wasn't just about posture or appearance; it was about composure, self-control, and the quiet strength that comes from knowing who you are and what you represent. It shaped not only how you acted in the field, but how you approached every challenge placed in front of you.

Spiritual bearing follows many of the same principles. It becomes visible in the way you interact with the people around you, how you treat others, how you respond when irritation rises, how you handle conflict or disagreement, and how you speak to your family in moments of stress or fatigue. It shows up in the way you extend kindness to strangers, offer patience to those who test your limits, and choose grace even when frustration would be easier. These moments reveal more about your spiritual maturity than any outward expression ever could.

Gentleness often gets mistaken for weakness, but it is actually one of the clearest signs of strength under control. It reflects a heart that is anchored, steady, and shaped by the character of Christ. When you demonstrate spiritual bearing, you're not putting on a performance; you're allowing the presence of Jesus within you to guide your responses and reshape your instincts.

Let that bearing shine today. Let it be seen in your words, your actions, your reactions, and your attitude. When Christ is living in you, His strength becomes the foundation for how you carry yourself in every moment, calm, steady, compassionate, and strong.

Prayer:
Jesus, shape my attitude. Let my words and actions reflect Your character.

Call to Action:

What attitude do you need God to shape today?

_____

_____

_____

_____

_____

Day 50: The Veteran's Gratitude

Scripture: *In every thing give thanks: for this is the will of God in Christ Jesus concerning you.*
1 Thessalonians 5:18

Gratitude has the power to shift the entire battlefield of the mind. Veterans often understand this in a unique way, because you've learned to appreciate the simple things, fresh air after being confined, a warm meal after going without, a safe place to sleep, the presence of family, and the gift of freedom. These everyday blessings become treasures when you've experienced life without them. But as the years move on, and responsibilities, pressures, or chronic health issues build up, it's easy for frustration, fatigue, or pain to bury that sense of gratitude. The things you once cherished can start to feel overshadowed by stress or weariness.

That's why Scripture doesn't tell you to be grateful for everything, but to be grateful in everything. Gratitude doesn't deny the reality of hardship. It doesn't ask you to pretend your struggles aren't real or that your valleys aren't difficult. Instead, gratitude repositions your heart so that the challenges don't consume your entire perspective. It reminds you that even in the midst of pain, God's goodness is still present, and blessings still surround you.

Take a moment to consider what your heart can give thanks for today. Perhaps it's your family, who loves you and relies on you. Maybe it's the simple fact that you're still here, still standing, still fighting. It could be your salvation, the assurance that God has claimed you as His own. It

might be your sense of purpose, your calling, or the steady presence of God who walks beside you in every season. These reminders don't erase your struggles, but they strengthen your spirit and steady your outlook.

Gratitude is a powerful tool for the soul. Practice it today, and let it reshape your inner battles with renewed hope and clarity.

Prayer:
Lord, open my eyes to Your blessings. Help me live with a grateful heart.

Call to Action:

What three things are you grateful for right now?

_____

_____

_____

_____

Day 51: When You Don't Feel Strong

Scripture: *My grace is sufficient for thee: for my strength is made perfect in weakness. 2 Corinthians 12:9*

Veterans often carry a lifelong expectation of strength. From the beginning of your service, you were trained to push through pain, to endure long beyond your limits, and to hold yourself together for the sake of others. You were the one people relied on, the steady one, the capable one, the one who didn't flinch even when everything hurt. That mindset stays with you long after the uniform comes off, and it can make weakness feel like something to hide or power through.

But God teaches something very different. He says His power doesn't wait for you to feel strong; it shines brightest in the moments when your strength runs out. The days when fatigue weighs heavy after years of poor sleep. The sinus flare-ups that make even simple tasks feel exhausting. The battle with sleep apnea that leaves you waking tired no matter how long you rest. The worn-out joints from years of ruck marches and physical strain. The tinnitus that never stops ringing. The headaches, back pain, or dizziness that come and go without warning. The anxious moments that tighten your chest. The low-energy seasons where motivation feels impossible. None of these struggles are failures, and they're not signs that something is wrong with your faith.

These moments simply reveal that you are human, and they create space for God's strength to show up in ways you could never manufacture on your own. You don't have to

hide your weakness from Him. You don't need to pretend you're fine when your body, mind, or emotions are worn thin. God isn't asking you to be invincible. He's inviting you to bring your fragility to Him, trusting that He can carry what you cannot.

He has never asked you to be the strongest person in the room. He has asked you to be the most surrendered, to let Him work through every limitation, every weary moment, and every place where your strength ends. In those very places, His power becomes unmistakably real.

Prayer:
Father, I give You my weakness. Let Your strength shine through me today.

Call to Action:

Where do you need God's strength the most today?

_____

_____

_____

_____

_____

Day 52: Enemy Territory

Scripture: *Be not overcome of evil, but overcome evil with good.   Romans 12:21*

There were places overseas where the atmosphere felt heavy,
like you were walking through unseen danger.

Some situations today feel the same way.
A difficult workplace.
A strained home environment.
A stressful meeting.
A spiritual darkness that's hard to name.

Evil still moves.
But goodness overpowers it.

When you walk into a room with Christ in you, the atmosphere changes.

Light enters enemy territory.

Your presence, filled with the Spirit, becomes a force for good that pushes back darkness.

Don't underestimate what God does through you.

Prayer:
Lord, help me carry Your light into every dark place I enter today.

Call to Action:

What dark place can you bring God's light into today?

_____

_____

_____

_____

_____

Day 53: "Hold Fast"

Scripture: *Let us hold fast the profession of our faith without wavering.   Hebrews 10:23*

"Hold fast" is a phrase that sailors and soldiers understand deeply. It's more than a command, it's a mindset. It means tightening your grip when conditions get rough, refusing to quit when the pressure intensifies, and standing firm when everything around you is unstable. It's the kind of determination that gets you through storms, battles, long nights, and moments when your strength feels like it's slipping. You learned not to let go, not to collapse, and not to surrender to fear, even when quitting would have been easier.

Spiritually, God calls you to live with that same resolve. He tells you to hold fast to hope, not the fragile kind of hope that depends on circumstances or emotions, but a hope anchored in His unchanging faithfulness. This is hope that doesn't shift when life gets harder, hope that doesn't crumble when disappointment comes, and hope that stays steady because it rests on the character of God rather than the chaos around you.

There will be moments when circumstances shake you, when fear creeps in quietly, or when your prayers seem to linger unanswered far longer than expected. Those are the moments when God whispers the same words you once heard in uniform: Hold fast. Keep your grip on the promises He has spoken. Steady your heart on the truth of who He is.

God has carried you through battles, hardships, and seasons you didn't think you would survive. He has never failed

you, not once. And the God who has proven Himself faithful time and time again will not start failing now. Hold fast to Him, because He is holding fast to you.

Prayer:
Lord, help me hold fast to Your promises. Strengthen my hope today.

Call to Action:

What promise of God do you need to hold onto?

_____

_____

_____

_____

_____

Day 54: Overcoming Fear

Scripture: *For God hath not given us the spirit of fear; but of power, and of love, and of a sound mind.*
2 Timothy 1:7

Fear is a powerful enemy, one that doesn't always look like the dangers you faced in uniform. When you were in real-world danger, what you felt wasn't fear, it was courage under pressure, a steady resolve that pushed you to act even when the situation was intense. That kind of strength comes from training, discipline, and the instinct to protect. But the fear God warns about is different. It's the kind that quietly slips into the heart and tries to paralyze your spirit long before a battle ever begins.

This kind of fear shows up in the quiet moments, fear of the future and what might come, fear of failure or not living up to the expectations of others, fear of sickness or worsening health, fear that you're not enough, fear of letting your family down, or fear of walking into an uncertain tomorrow without a clear path. These fears can weigh heavily on a person, often more than physical danger ever could. But none of them come from God. He doesn't speak in the language of fear. He doesn't motivate through anxiety. He doesn't burden you with dread or discouragement.

Instead, God gives you strength that equips you to face life with confidence. He gives you power to stand firm, love that steadies your relationships and your heart, and a sound mind capable of clarity, wisdom, and peace. These gifts are meant to override the fears that try to creep in. You don't have to entertain every fearful thought that knocks on the door of your mind. You can recognize it, name it, and still

choose not to let it inside. With God's presence guiding you and His peace guarding you, fear loses its authority.

Fear may knock, but by God's strength, you never have to open the door.

Prayer:
Father, replace my fears with Your power, love, and peace today.

Call to Action:

What fear will you surrender to God right now?

_____

_____

_____

_____

_____

Day 55: The Importance of Small Wins

Scripture: *For who hath despised the day of small things? Zechariah 4:10*

In training, you were never thrown straight into the hardest task on day one. You started with the basics, learning the fundamentals, mastering simple movements, building endurance in small increments. Those early wins, even though they seemed minor at the time, created the foundation that eventually led you to bigger victories. Progress came through repetition, consistency, and small steps that built confidence and ability over time.

Your spiritual life works in much the same way. Small wins matter more than most people realize. Opening your Bible and reading even a single chapter plants truth in your heart. Taking a few minutes to pray strengthens your connection with God. Encouraging one person lifts someone else's spirit and shapes your own. Showing patience in a moment when irritation rises builds character. Serving in quiet, unseen ways develops humility and faithfulness. These moments may feel small, but together they form spiritual momentum that grows stronger day after day.

You don't need to transform into a spiritual powerhouse overnight. Growth doesn't happen through giant leaps, it happens through steady, faithful steps forward. All God asks is that you take the next step, however small it may seem. Every piece of progress, every moment of effort, every step toward Him is noticed, valued, and strengthened by His grace.

Keep moving forward. God honors every bit of progress you make.

Prayer:
Lord, help me celebrate small steps of faith. Build my strength through daily victories.

Call to Action:

What is one small step forward you can take today?

_____

_____

_____

_____

_____

Day 56: The Sound of Freedom

Scripture: *Where the Spirit of the Lord is, there is liberty.*
2 Corinthians 3:17

Veterans understand freedom in a way that goes far deeper than a simple definition. You've been in places where freedom didn't exist, where people lived under oppression, fear, or instability. You've served to protect the freedoms others take for granted, standing in the gap so your family and country could enjoy safety and opportunity. You've witnessed the cost of freedom, its sacrifices, its weight, and the lives forever marked by its defense. That experience gives you a perspective most will never comprehend.

But even with all that, spiritual freedom reaches further still. It's the kind of freedom that lifts burdens the world cannot touch. It releases the heart from guilt that tries to cling to your conscience. It breaks chains of addiction and long-standing struggles that feel too heavy to fight alone. It silences fear and the voice that whispers you're not enough. It removes shame that tries to define you, and it severs the grip of a past that has followed you for years. This is freedom that doesn't depend on circumstances, achievements, or strength, it rests entirely on Christ.

And because it comes from Him, this freedom can't be stolen, revoked, or threatened. No attack from the enemy, no failure on your part, and no hardship you endure can take it away. It is secured by the power of Jesus, anchored in His sacrifice, and protected by His presence.

Let His Spirit breathe that freedom into every corner of your life today, into your mind, your memories, your health, your relationships, and the places still recovering from old battles. Walk in the kind of freedom only Christ can give, knowing it is yours fully and forever.

Prayer:
Holy Spirit, fill me with Your freedom. Break every chain in my life.

Call to Action:

What area of your life needs Christ's freedom?

_____

_____

_____

_____

_____

Day 57: When Strength Feels Far Away

Scripture: *But they that wait upon the Lord shall renew their strength. Isaiah 40:31*

There are days when strength feels impossibly far away, days when simply getting out of bed feels like a victory in itself. Your energy runs low, your lungs feel tight or heavy, and your sinuses make breathing feel more like work than something automatic. The nights when sleep refuses to come leave you dragging through the morning, and the stress that sits in your chest seems to grow heavier with every passing hour. On days like these, it's easy to wonder how much longer you can keep going at all.

But God offers a promise that reaches far beyond physical endurance. He assures you that renewal is available, not just for your body, but for your spirit. He sees the weariness others overlook. He understands the fatigue that settles deeper than muscle and bone. And in those places where you feel weak, depleted, or overwhelmed, He steps in with strength that doesn't come from human effort.

God lifts the weary when they can't lift themselves. He restores the tired heart that feels stretched thin. He strengthens those whose spirits feel faint, giving them what they need one moment at a time. You were never expected to soar on your own. The image of rising on wings like eagles isn't something you achieve by pushing harder, it's something God does in you and for you.

He is the one who carries you to that altitude, who lifts you above the weight of your circumstances, and who breathes

renewed strength into your spirit when you feel empty. Place your hope in Him, even on the days when that hope feels fragile. As you lean into His presence, strength will rise, quietly, steadily, and faithfully, until you find yourself standing again with renewed power.

Prayer:
Lord, renew my strength today. Lift me above what wears me down.

Call to Action:

How can you invite God to renew your strength today?

_____

_____

_____

_____

_____

Day 58: Learning to Trust Again

Scripture: *He is a buckler to all those that trust in him.*
Psalm 18:30

Trust is something veterans understand on a deeper level than most people ever will. You learned early on that trust isn't automatic, it's earned through experience, through proven loyalty, through shared hardship. You trusted the ones who consistently showed up, the ones who covered your blind spots, the ones who stayed steady when everything around you was uncertain. Trust was built in the field, in the heat of pressure, in the quiet moments when someone else's reliability meant the difference between safety and danger.

Because of that, trusting God can sometimes feel complicated. Not because He has ever failed you, but because people have. Broken promises, betrayal, disappointment, abandonment, these wounds make it hard to open your heart, even to the One who's never hurt you. Human failures have a way of creating spiritual hesitation, and it's easy to project the flaws of others onto God.

But God is not like the people who let you down. He has never failed you, not once in your entire life. He has never betrayed your confidence, never walked away when things became difficult, never lied to you, and never shifted His character with changing seasons. His nature is constant. His loyalty is unwavering. His promises hold steady even when your circumstances don't.

When you take refuge in Him, you're placing your trust in Someone who has already proven Himself faithful long before you even realized how much you needed Him. Trust doesn't appear overnight; it grows slowly, step by step, through moments of choosing to believe even when feelings are uncertain. And the incredible thing is this: every single step you take toward trusting God is met with His faithfulness. He reinforces that trust with compassion, with provision, with peace, and with a steady presence that never falters.

Let your trust in Him grow at its own pace. As you lean into Him, you will find that He is more reliable than anyone you have ever known, and He will meet every step you take with perfect, unchanging faithfulness.

Prayer:
Lord, rebuild my trust. Help me take refuge in Your unchanging character.

Call to Action:

Where do you need to trust God more deeply?

_____

_____

_____

_____

_____

Day 59: Inspecting Your Perimeter

Scripture: *Search me, O God, and know my heart. Psalm 139:23*

Perimeter checks were a normal and essential part of military life. You walked the lines, examined every corner, cleared the blind spots, and made sure there were no weak spots an enemy could exploit. Those checks weren't optional, they were a protective discipline, a way to stay ahead of danger rather than react to it. You understood that vigilance was part of survival, and a secure perimeter meant everyone under your care was safer.

Your spiritual life needs that same level of intentional attention. Just as you once checked fences, paths, and shadows, you now need to examine the unseen areas of your heart and mind. Asking God to look into your attitudes, habits, motives, relationships, and personal weak points isn't about inviting shame or condemnation, it's about inviting protection. You're asking Him to shine light on areas where the enemy might try to slip in quietly, long before the attack becomes obvious.

A secure perimeter keeps threats out in the field, and a clean heart keeps your spirit steady and strong. When you allow God to inspect the places you can't see clearly, He reveals what needs healing, strengthens what needs reinforcement, and guards what matters most. His insight reaches deeper than your own self-awareness, catching vulnerabilities you might overlook, and helping you grow in ways that protect your walk with Him.

Invite God into that inspection. Let Him walk the perimeter of your heart. He sees what you miss, understands what you carry, and knows exactly how to fortify the areas that need strengthening. With His help, your spiritual defenses stay strong, your heart stays clear, and your faith remains steady in every season.

Prayer:
Lord, search my heart. Reveal anything that needs to change and help me grow.

Call to Action:

What boundary do you need to strengthen?

_____

_____

_____

_____

_____

Day 60: Blessed Are the Peacemakers

Scripture: *Blessed are the peacemakers: for they shall be called the children of God.   Matthew 5:9*

Veterans understand conflict in ways most people never will, but you also understand the rare and precious value of peace. You've seen the cost of its absence, the tension, the destruction, the uncertainty that fills the void when peace is nowhere to be found. That experience gave you a deeper appreciation for what true peace feels like and why it matters so much. Because of that, you now carry a unique perspective into your everyday life.

God doesn't just call you to enjoy peace; He calls you to be a peacemaker. There's a big difference between keeping peace and making peace. A peacekeeper often avoids conflict, stays quiet, or steps around tension to preserve comfort. But a peacemaker steps into difficult spaces with the intention of restoring what's broken. It's someone who brings calm where emotions run high, who introduces clarity where confusion has taken root, and who carries Christ's presence into situations that desperately need it.

This calling shows up in the everyday places of your life, in your home when tempers rise or misunderstandings appear, in your workplace where stress can strain relationships, in your church where unity must be protected, and in your marriage where patience and grace are essential. It even shows up in your own mind, where inner storms sometimes rage and peace feels distant. Being a peacemaker means allowing God's peace to settle in you so deeply that it naturally begins to flow outward to others.

Wherever you go, you carry Christ's peace into tense moments. You bring steadiness into chaos, speak truth into confusion, and help pull people together when division threatens to take hold. This isn't a small task, it's a Kingdom mission, and it's one God has specifically equipped you to fulfill because of what you've lived through and who you've become.

This is your mission today: to be someone who creates peace in places that lack it, reflecting the heart of Christ with every step you take.

Prayer:
Jesus, fill me with Your peace. Help me bring that peace everywhere I go.

Call to Action:

Where can you intentionally bring peace today?

_____

_____

_____

_____

_____

Day 61: When the Road Gets Rough

Scripture: *The Lord shall fight for you, and ye shall hold your peace. Exodus 14:14*

Some missions took you across rough terrain, thick sand that swallowed your steps, uneven ground that tested your balance, and heat so intense it drained your strength faster than you could replenish it. Yet you pushed forward because stopping wasn't an option. You adapted, endured, and advanced, even when the environment fought against you. That determination became part of who you are.

Life brings its own rugged terrain, the kind that doesn't show up on a map but still makes the journey difficult. There are seasons when prayers remain unanswered longer than you hoped, when unexpected bad news hits like a sudden ambush, when finances tighten and create pressure you can't seem to escape, when health issues refuse to improve no matter how hard you try, and when discouragement sneaks in quietly, weakening your motivation from the inside out. These moments feel like uphill marches where every step takes more effort than the last.

Yet even in these stretches of rough road, God has a simple but profound message: you don't have to fight every battle by yourself. Sometimes the most faithful action you can take is not pressing harder, but pausing long enough to let Him move. Stillness isn't inaction or defeat, it's a deliberate choice to trust that God is doing what you cannot see. It's stepping back so He can step forward, recognizing

that His strength is greater than your exhaustion, and His timing wiser than your urgency.

Stillness is not surrender. It is trust. It is the quiet confidence that God is working in the background, even when the terrain is rough and the path unclear. When you choose to be still, you're not giving up the mission, you're placing it in the hands of the One who knows exactly how to carry you through it.

Prayer:
Lord, help me be still and trust You to fight what I cannot fight myself.

Call to Action:

What situation do you need God to fight for you?

_____

_____

_____

_____

_____

Day 62: The Weight of Responsibility

Scripture: *Cast thy burden upon the Lord, and he shall sustain thee.   Psalm 55:22*

Veterans carry responsibility in a way that sets them apart. You were trained to step up when others stepped back, to fix what was broken, to protect those around you, and to hold your world together even when the pressure felt unbearable. That conditioning doesn't disappear after service, it follows you into civilian life, into your family, into your work, and into every quiet moment where you feel the weight of being the one who must "hold it all together." Even when you're exhausted, overwhelmed, or silently struggling, something in you pushes to keep carrying the load because that's what you were taught to do.

But God never designed you to carry every burden by yourself. His plan was never for you to be the strongest person in every room or the one who solves every crisis. You don't have to be the constant protector who absorbs every blow. You don't have to hold your family's future together with your bare hands. And you certainly don't have to pretend the load isn't heavy when it is pulling you to your knees. God didn't call you to be invincible, He called you to be His.

He is the one who sustains you. Not your physical strength, not the discipline you learned in uniform, not the willpower you've relied on for decades. Those things have carried you far, but they were never meant to carry you forever. God Himself is the strength that holds you upright when your

own strength runs out. He is the foundation beneath your feet, the support beneath your burdens, and the peace beneath your anxieties.

Let Him carry the weight you've been holding so tightly. Release the burdens you've tucked away in silence. Allow Him to step into the places where you've been pushing through alone. When you let God shoulder the load, you make room to breathe again, to rest, to heal, and to rediscover the peace He's been offering all along.

Prayer:
Father, take the burdens I've been carrying. Sustain me with Your strength.

Call to Action:

Which responsibility do you need to surrender to God's care?

_____

_____

_____

_____

_____

Day 63: Spiritual Field Manual

Scripture: *All scripture is given by inspiration of God, and is profitable for doctrine, for reproof, for correction, for instruction in righteousness. 2 Timothy 3:16*

Every soldier knows the importance of manuals. You relied on them from the very beginning, training manuals that explained the fundamentals, equipment manuals that taught you how to operate and maintain your gear, and operational guides that outlined procedures essential for safety and success. These resources weren't optional; they were lifelines. They gave clarity in confusion, direction in uncertainty, and confidence in moments when hesitation could cost dearly. You opened them with intention because you understood that what you learned from them could save your life or the life of someone beside you.

The Bible serves as your spiritual field manual in much the same way. It is not just a book of stories or inspirational sayings, it is God's instruction, correction, and preparation for every mission He places in front of you. It teaches you how to stand firm when life feels unstable, how to navigate conflict without losing your peace, how to resist spiritual attacks, and how to live with purpose, hope, and strength. It equips you with wisdom for decisions, comfort for hardship, and courage for the battles you never saw coming.

Approach Scripture the same way you once approached your gear: carefully, with respect for its importance; deliberately, knowing that what you take in will shape your readiness; and regularly, because a tool unused becomes

ineffective over time. As you read, the Word strengthens your mind, anchors your heart, and prepares your spirit for whatever lies ahead. It reinforces truth when lies try to creep in and provides stability when emotions or circumstances shift unexpectedly.

Just as you would never step into a mission unprepared, don't step into your day without God's Word. Let it be the manual that steadies your hands, sharpens your awareness, and equips you for the spiritual battles you face. Don't leave home without it, it is essential gear for the journey.

Prayer:
Lord, help me love Your Word and rely on it as my guide in every situation.

Call to Action:

What Scripture will you meditate on today?

_____

_____

_____

_____

_____

Day 64: When Strength Isn't Enough

Scripture: *Not by might, nor by power, but by my spirit, saith the Lord of hosts.* Zechariah 4:6

You've leaned on strength for as long as you can remember, strength of body, strength of mind, strength of will. Physical strength carried you through demanding tasks. Mental strength pushed you to stay alert and steady when situations grew intense. Emotional strength helped you shoulder responsibilities others couldn't see. Discipline kept you moving forward when everything in you felt exhausted, and determination allowed you to finish what you started, no matter the cost. Relying on your own strength became a way of life, something almost instinctive.

But sooner or later, life brings battles that simply won't yield to willpower. Addiction doesn't respond to toughness. Fear digs in deeper the more you try to out-muscle it. Anxiety refuses to back down just because you tell it to. Health struggles, chronic pain, fatigue, sleep issues, sinus flare-ups, or old injuries that flare without warning, don't bow to determination. And spiritual battles, the unseen pressures and wounds from your past that still echo in your present, cannot be conquered through sheer grit. These battles run deeper than muscle, deeper than mindset, deeper than anything human strength can resolve.

That's why God gives His people the power of the Holy Spirit. The Spirit does what human effort can never accomplish. He breaks chains you've tried for years to loosen. He calms the storms that rage inside your chest. He

brings healing to wounds you thought time had buried. He strengthens you in places your natural strength simply cannot reach. Where your power stops, His begins, and there is no limit to what He can do.

When you surrender the fight to Him, not giving up, but handing over what was never meant to be carried alone, God starts moving mountains that have stood in your way for far too long. He lifts burdens, opens doors, restores peace, and brings victories that reflect His power rather than your exhaustion.

Your strength has taken you far, but God's Spirit can take you further than strength ever could. Let Him step into the battles that outmatch you. He is more than able to carry what you cannot.

Prayer:
Holy Spirit, fight the battles I can't fight. Work in me with Your power.

Call to Action:

Where do you need to rely on God's Spirit instead of your strength?

_____

_____

_____

_____

_____

Day 65: Keeping Your Edge

Scripture: *Stir up the gift of God, which is in thee.*
2 Timothy 1:6

A good soldier knows the importance of staying sharp, mentally, emotionally, and physically. You trained to keep your edge, to stay alert, prepared, and ready for whatever the mission demanded. Letting yourself grow dull was never an option, because lives depended on your readiness. That mindset doesn't disappear when the uniform comes off, and spiritually, it matters just as much.

Your spiritual edge can dull over time if you're not intentional. Faith that once burned brightly can settle into routine. The gifts God placed inside you can sit unused, not because they've disappeared, but because life has a way of pulling your attention in a thousand different directions. Even your calling, the purpose God wove into your life, can get buried under responsibilities, fatigue, or seasons where you simply feel disconnected. But just because something feels quiet doesn't mean it's gone. The embers of your faith are still alive, even if they seem faint, and God is more than capable of fanning them back into a strong, steady flame.

That renewal doesn't happen overnight; it grows through small, simple, intentional steps. Worship softens the heart and draws you closer to God's presence. Scripture strengthens your mind and brings clarity into areas that feel uncertain. Serving others awakens purpose and reminds you that God still works through you. Prayer reconnects your spirit to the One who empowers you. And stepping back into the things God uniquely created you to do brings those dormant gifts back to life. None of these actions are grand gestures; they are steady rhythms that sharpen your spiritual edge again.

You are not past your usefulness. Nothing God placed inside you has expired. Your gifts still burn within you, waiting for breath and attention. Let God reignite what has been quiet. Take the small steps that fan those embers back into flame. Your spiritual strength can return stronger than before, ready for the missions still ahead.

Prayer:
Lord, reignite my gifts. Restore my spiritual edge so I can serve You boldly.

Call to Action:

What spiritual gift or skill do you need to reignite?

_____

_____

_____

_____

_____

Day 66: Staying in Formation

Scripture: *And let us consider one another to provoke unto love and to good works.   Hebrews 10:24*

In the military, formation isn't just a strategy, it's a lifeline. You learned early on that you don't fight well on your own. You advance together, cover each other's blind spots, and move as a unified force. Formation provides protection, direction, and strength. It keeps you from becoming an easy target and ensures that no one is left isolated or exposed.

Spiritually, the same principle holds true. Isolation is dangerous in ways that aren't always obvious at first. When you drift away from fellowship, your strength slowly fades. When you disconnect from your church, the support that once held you steady becomes harder to find. When you avoid community, you lose the covering and encouragement that God designed to sustain you during difficult seasons. No believer was meant to walk alone, and no soldier of faith thrives in solitude.

You need a spiritual formation just as much as you needed your military one. You need brothers and sisters who will pray for you, stand with you, challenge you, and remind you of truth when your mind grows weary. You need a church family that surrounds you with love, accountability, and encouragement. You need a circle of support, people who know your battles, respect your journey, and walk beside you with loyalty and grace.

When you move together, you grow stronger. When you grow together, you deepen your endurance. And when you fight together, you overcome battles you would never defeat alone. Let God place you in the formation you need.

There is strength in community, power in unity, and protection in walking with others who share your mission and your faith.

Prayer:
Father, help me stay connected to the body of Christ. Surround me with strong, faithful believers.

Call to Action:

Who do you need to reconnect with spiritually?

_____

_____

_____

_____

_____

Day 67: The Veteran's Integrity

Scripture: *The integrity of the upright shall guide them. Proverbs 11:3*

Integrity was drilled into you from the very beginning, do the right thing, even when no one sees, even when it costs you something, even when cutting corners would be easier. It wasn't just a rule; it was a standard that shaped who you became as a service member and as a person. That training built a foundation of character that others recognized and respected, often without you ever needing to say a word about it.

God places a tremendous value on integrity as well. Your honesty, your reliability, and the consistency of your character become a kind of testimony that reaches further than you realize. People trust you because your actions match your words. They feel safe around you because they know you mean what you say. In a world filled with empty promises and shifting values, a person of integrity stands out like a steady lighthouse, immovable, dependable, and unmistakably genuine.

Integrity becomes a guide for your decisions, helping you choose what is right even when the path is difficult. It protects your reputation, shielding you from consequences that come when others compromise. And above all, integrity honors God. It reflects His nature, truthful, faithful, and unchanging, through the way you conduct your daily life.

So stay true today. In your conversations, let your words be honest and uplifting. In your choices, keep your heart aligned with what you know is right. In private moments, when no one else sees, remain faithful to the standards God has planted in you. Integrity is more than a virtue, it is your armor, your protection, and one of the greatest strengths you carry.

Wear it proudly, because it shows the world not only who you are, but who God is within you.

Prayer:
Lord, strengthen my integrity. Help me honor You in every decision.

Call to Action:

Where do you need to make the honest, right choice today?

_____

_____

_____

_____

_____

Day 68: When You Feel Isolated

Scripture: *I will never leave thee, nor forsake thee.*
Hebrews 13:5

Some of the hardest moments veterans face aren't tied to danger, deployment, or high-pressure situations, they emerge quietly, long after the uniform is folded away. Isolation has a way of sneaking in during the still moments, when you feel misunderstood by people who can't relate to what you've lived through, or when you're surrounded by others yet still feel disconnected inside. It's the kind of loneliness that settles deep, making you feel unseen, unheard, or emotionally distant even in a room full of people. That kind of isolation is heavy, and it can make you believe you're fighting your battles on your own.

But isolation doesn't alter God's nearness. Your feelings may shift, your energy may fade, and your sense of connection to others may fluctuate, but His presence stays constant. He is closer than your next breath, closer than your thoughts, closer than the emotions that rise and fall within you. God doesn't step back when your mood dips or when discouragement lingers. He doesn't withdraw when you're tired, overwhelmed, or unsure of how to reach out. He certainly doesn't remain silent when your heart feels tangled in struggles you can't explain.

He is with you, fully, completely, continually. His presence surrounds you in moments of confidence and moments of confusion, in seasons of strength and seasons of weariness. He doesn't wait for you to "pull it together" before He

draws near. He meets you exactly where you are, even in the places you'd rather hide.

You may feel alone at times, but you are never truly alone. God remains closer, steadier, and more faithful than your emotions will ever tell you. His presence fills the isolation, and His companionship anchors your soul when the world feels distant.

Prayer:
Lord, remind me of Your presence today. Help me feel Your nearness in moments of isolation.

Call to Action:

Who can you reach out to so you don't walk alone?

_____

_____

_____

_____

_____

Day 69: Forward March

Scripture: *...forgetting those things which are behind, and reaching forth unto those things which are before, I press toward the mark... Philippians 3:13–14*

Marching forward was never optional in the military. Whether your feet ached, your muscles burned, or your spirit felt worn down, you kept moving. Stopping wasn't part of the mission. You learned to push through fatigue, discomfort, and discouragement because forward motion was part of survival, and part of becoming who you were trained to be.

Spiritually, God calls you to that same kind of steady movement. He asks you to keep marching even when the past whispers your old mistakes, even when failures try to haunt your thoughts, and even when regret attempts to drag you backward into seasons you've already outgrown. The past is persistent, but it is not your commander. It does not have authority to determine your direction anymore.

Your past is behind you, fully, permanently, completely. God has already dealt with it, forgiven it, and released you from its grip. Your mission, your purpose, and your future are ahead of you. God is leading you toward things more meaningful and more fulfilling than anything you left behind: deeper peace, stronger faith, healthier relationships, and a calling that grows richer with time. He isn't interested in returning you to old battles; He is guiding you toward new ground that reflects His promises and your growth.

So press on. Move forward with determination, one step at a time. Don't turn your head to stare at what's already been

buried. God is not behind you, He is in front of you, inviting you into the next chapter of strength, healing, and purpose. Don't look back; what awaits you is far better than what you've left behind.

Prayer:
Lord, help me release the past and press forward into the future You have for me.

Call to Action:

What part of your past do you need to stop looking back at?

_____

_____

_____

_____

_____

Day 70: A Warrior's Peace

Scripture: *Peace I leave with you, my peace I give unto you: not as the world giveth, give I unto you.* John 14:27

Peace lands differently for someone who has truly known danger. After experiencing moments where safety was uncertain and silence held tension instead of comfort, you learn to appreciate quiet in a way others can't fully understand. You cherish the simple moments when nothing threatens you. You value safe places, steady routines, and environments where your guard can finally come down. Stillness becomes more than a pause, it becomes a gift.

But Jesus offers a peace that goes even deeper than the quiet you've come to cherish. His peace calms the mind when thoughts start racing. It steadies the heart when emotions feel unpredictable. It guards the spirit when life becomes overwhelming. This peace doesn't depend on circumstances behaving themselves, and it doesn't disappear when stress or uncertainty rise. It's not fragile, not fleeting, not something that can be shaken loose by a hard day or a difficult season.

Christ's peace is solid, immovable even when the world around you shifts. It becomes an anchor that keeps you grounded when storms hit, a shield that protects your spirit when pressure builds, and a steadying presence that keeps you from being pulled into fear or chaos. A warrior who carries that kind of peace is truly unstoppable. They remain calm under pressure, steady when others feel shaken, and anchored in truth no matter what threatens their footing.

Let His peace surround and guard you today. Allow it to settle into the places where tension still lingers and fill the

corners of your life where rest feels distant. Christ's peace is your strength, your stability, and your protection, far deeper and stronger than anything the world can offer.

Prayer:
Jesus, fill me with Your peace. Let it steady me in every circumstance.

Call to Action:

What situation needs God's peace right now?

_____

_____

_____

_____

_____

Day 71: The Veteran's Endurance

Scripture: *But let patience have her perfect work. James 1:4*

Endurance was woven into every part of your training. You learned it through long marches that tested your legs and lungs, through grueling PT that pushed your limits, and through tough days when quitting simply wasn't an option. Those experiences didn't just strengthen your body, they strengthened your resolve. You discovered that endurance is built one difficult step at a time, and that pushing forward when everything in you wants to stop develops a kind of toughness nothing else can produce.

Spiritually, God uses endurance in much the same way. Every trial you face, every hardship you push through, and every season that stretches your patience is doing more than creating discomfort, it's producing something meaningful inside you. Perseverance grows when you keep believing even when the answers are slow. Character deepens when you choose integrity in the middle of difficulty. Maturity forms when you trust God instead of rushing ahead on your own. Wisdom develops as you look back and see how God used what felt painful to guide you into something better.

Endurance is not about needless suffering or proving your toughness to God. It's about shaping, God shaping you into someone stronger, more grounded, and more faithful than you were before the trial began. He uses endurance to refine your heart, sharpen your focus, and prepare you for the bigger missions He has ahead.

So let endurance finish its work. Don't rush the process or assume the struggle means God is distant. He is shaping something powerful in you, something that will carry you into your next season with greater strength, deeper faith, and a steadier spirit than you've ever had before.

Prayer:
Father, give me strength to endure every trial. Shape me into Your image.

Call to Action:

Where do you need endurance to finish strong?

_____

_____

_____

_____

_____

Day 72: Your Life Has Meaning

Scripture: *Before I formed thee in the belly I knew thee. Jeremiah 1:5*

Sometimes veterans wrestle with a deep sense of meaning after their time in uniform ends. The mission changes, and the structure that once shaped every day seems to disappear overnight. The rhythm, the routine, the clear objectives, and the sense of belonging to something bigger than yourself can suddenly feel distant. What once guided your steps no longer defines your days, and that shift can leave you wondering where you fit and what your purpose looks like now. It's a quiet struggle many veterans carry but rarely speak about.

But God speaks directly into that uncertainty. He reminds you that your life still carries tremendous meaning. Nothing about your story has lost value. The experiences you've lived, the lessons you've learned, the strength you've built, and the compassion you've gained through hardship all matter deeply in His Kingdom. Your presence still makes a difference, to your family, your community, your church, and the people whose lives intersect with yours in ways you may never fully see.

God doesn't retire His soldiers. He redeploys them. Your mission hasn't ended; it has shifted into a new field of influence. You still carry purpose that only you can fulfill. You possess calling that God intends to use in powerful ways. Your influence stretches further than you realize, shaping lives through your character, your encouragement, your wisdom, and your example. Your value hasn't

diminished with time, it has matured, deepened, and taken on new weight.

You matter profoundly to God. And you matter to the people around you, even if they don't always know how to say it. Your story is still unfolding, and God is still writing meaningful chapters through your life.

Prayer:
Lord, remind me that my life still has purpose. Show me how I can serve You today.

Call to Action:

How can you live in your God-given purpose today?

_____

_____

_____

_____

_____

Day 73: When You Need Reinforcements

Scripture: *The Lord is my helper.   Hebrews 13:6*

A good soldier knows exactly when to call for backup. Experience taught you that running headfirst into danger alone isn't bravery, it's recklessness. Support exists for a reason. Calling for help isn't a sign of weakness; it's a sign of wisdom, strategy, and survival. You learned to trust your team, rely on reinforcements, and recognize that strength multiplies when others join the fight.

Spiritually, the same truth holds. You were never meant to face life's toughest moments by yourself. When temptation begins to creep in, when discouragement hits you harder than expected, when stress starts climbing faster than you can manage, when anxiety tightens its grip around your chest, or when sickness and fatigue weaken your body, these are not moments to push forward alone. They are signals, clear, unmistakable moments, inviting you to call for divine reinforcements.

God is your helper. Not reluctantly, as if your struggles are an inconvenience. Not occasionally, as if He only responds on certain days. But faithfully, every time you cry out. He moves toward you with a speed and certainty that surpasses even the most dependable soldier you ever served with. His support doesn't run out. His strength doesn't fade. His presence doesn't hesitate.

When you call for God's help, He steps into the battle with you. He brings clarity where confusion swirls, peace where panic rises, and power where your strength is drained. He

fortifies what feels weak and lifts what you can no longer carry.

You were never meant to fight alone. Call for backup. God stands ready, always, your greatest ally in every battle you face.

Prayer:
Lord, I need Your help today. Strengthen me with Your presence and power.

Call to Action:

Where do you need God's help most urgently?

_____

_____

_____

_____

_____

Day 74: The Value of Consistency

Scripture: *And let us not be weary in well doing. Galatians 6:9*

Great victories are rarely the result of one dramatic moment. More often, they're built through quiet, repeated steps, small decisions that accumulate over time until they form something strong, steady, and unshakable. You learned this lesson in the military. Consistency became part of your identity. You showed up even when you were exhausted. You followed through even when the task felt tedious. You stayed disciplined whether the day was easy or grueling. And you did the right thing not for applause, but because integrity demanded it, even when no one else was watching.

Spiritually, that same consistency becomes just as vital. A strong walk with God isn't formed through occasional effort; it's built through daily rhythms that anchor your heart. Praying regularly keeps your connection to God alive and personal. Reading Scripture renews your mind and strengthens your foundation. Serving others keeps your heart soft and your purpose active. Staying connected to church ensures you're surrounded by encouragement, accountability, and support. Walking in integrity, day in and day out, shapes your character into something dependable, authentic, and Christlike.

These habits may seem small, but they are the steady bricks of a resilient faith. They shape you quietly, often without your noticing. And even when progress feels slow, even

when you wonder if it's making a difference, God is working through every faithful step you take.

Keep doing good. Keep showing up. Keep practicing the disciplines that strengthen your spirit. Great victories are built slowly, but they last far longer because of it.

Prayer:
Father, make me a consistent man of faith. Strengthen my daily habits of obedience.

Call to Action:

What daily habit can you commit to this week?

_____

_____

_____

_____

_____

Day 75: God's Mercy in Every Morning

Scripture: *They are new every morning.*
Lamentations 3:23

Every morning arrives with a quiet gift, a fresh start, a chance to breathe again, a clean slate washed in grace, and a mercy renewed before you even open your eyes. The struggles of yesterday don't carry the authority to shape who you are today. Yesterday's failures that replay in your mind, yesterday's worries that tightened your chest, yesterday's mistakes that still sting, and yesterday's burdens that felt too heavy to carry, none of them have the right to define this new day God has placed in front of you.

God's mercy resets the battlefield every single morning. It wipes away the debris of yesterday's battles and gives you new footing, new strength, and a renewed sense of hope. No matter how exhausted you felt when you finally collapsed into bed, no matter how discouraged your thoughts became as the night grew quiet, and no matter what wound or heartbreak you've been trying to process, today does not begin where yesterday ended. It begins with mercy.

And mercy is stronger than exhaustion. It's stronger than regret. It's stronger than anxiety, disappointment, or the struggles you carried into the night. Mercy gives you room to breathe, to reset, and to rise again, not in your own strength, but in God's.

This morning is a gift. God meets you in it with compassion, forgiveness, and strength that is new, not

recycled, not leftover, but fresh for the battles and blessings ahead. Whatever today holds, you do not face it empty. You begin with mercy, and mercy is enough to carry you forward.

Prayer:
Lord, thank You for fresh mercy today. Help me walk in the freedom You give each morning.

Call to Action:

What fresh start do you need to embrace today?

_____

_____

_____

_____

_____

Day 76: The Veteran's Courage

Scripture: *Be of good courage, and he shall strengthen your heart, all ye that hope in the Lord.   Psalm 31:24*

Courage didn't always look like the dramatic moments people imagine when they think of military heroes. More often, it showed up in small, unseen ways. Some days, courage meant simply getting out of bed after a long night. It meant showing up for duty when your body ached or your mind was exhausted. It meant doing the next right thing even when motivation was low and the path forward wasn't clear. The courage you lived out daily wasn't loud or flashy, it was steady, determined, and deeply rooted.

Spiritual courage follows that same quiet pattern. It isn't always about grand acts of faith. Sometimes it's the courage to whisper a prayer when you don't feel spiritual at all. It's choosing to trust God when fear wants to take control. It's deciding to love again even when past wounds make you want to withdraw. It's taking another step forward when memories from the past reach up and try to hold you in place. This kind of courage isn't celebrated by crowds, but heaven sees it clearly, and God honors it deeply.

Waiting on the Lord is often misunderstood as passivity or weakness, but it's actually one of the purest forms of courage. It takes strength to pause when everything in you wants answers now. It takes faith to remain steady when God's timing unfolds slower than your expectations. It takes trust to believe He is working when you can't see movement on the surface.

Let your heart take courage today. Remind yourself that God has never been late, never been idle, and never once failed to keep His promises. Your courage, quiet or bold, small or significant, matters deeply to Him. And He will meet every courageous step with His unwavering faithfulness.

Prayer:
Lord, strengthen my heart with courage as I wait on You.

Call to Action:

What courageous step do you need to take today?

_____

_____

_____

_____

_____

Day 77: God's Strength in Your Weak Places

Scripture: *The Lord is the strength of my life.*
Psalm 27:1

Some parts of you still feel solid, steady, capable, and grounded from years of discipline and hard-earned resilience. But other parts feel worn down, stretched thin by time, stress, and the physical toll of life after service. The sleep issues that leave you dragging through the day, the chronic sinus problems that make breathing feel like a task, the joint pain that reminds you of everything your body has carried, the fatigue that settles into your bones, and the stress that weighs on your shoulders, these aren't small inconveniences. They chip away at your energy and often at your confidence, wearing on both the mind and the body of a veteran who has already endured so much.

Yet even in the places where you feel weakest, God's strength remains unchanged. Your physical limitations don't limit Him. Your mental exhaustion doesn't slow Him down. Your spiritual discouragement doesn't push Him away. His strength operates on a different level, one that isn't restricted by your body, your health, or your emotional reserves. His grace continues to flow into your life, unhindered by the very things that overwhelm you. And His power is not diminished just because you feel drained.

In fact, your weakness doesn't repel God at all, it draws His strength toward you. Where you feel fragile, He brings stability. Where you feel inadequate, He supplies more than enough. Where you feel burdened, He offers rest. God

doesn't stand back and wait for you to pull yourself together; He steps into the very cracks where you feel vulnerable.

Invite Him into those weak places today, the physical pain, the tired moments, the emotional strain, the spiritual dryness. Those are the spaces where His strength shines brightest, and where His presence becomes unmistakably real.

Prayer:
Father, be my strength where I am weak. Fill the places that feel empty with Your power.

Call to Action:

What weakness will you invite God into?

_____

_____

_____

_____

_____

Day 78: The Call to Advance

Scripture: *Arise, get thee out…   Genesis 31:13*

There were moments in your service when the only command that mattered was a simple, unmistakable word: **advance**. There was no room for hesitation, no space for debate, and no time for explanations. You didn't need a full briefing or detailed reasoning, you just moved. Your training, discipline, and trust in leadership pushed you forward, step after step, even when the terrain was uncertain or the outcome unclear. Movement itself became an act of obedience and courage.

God often speaks in that same quiet but unmistakably firm way. His voice doesn't always come with long explanations or a roadmap. Sometimes He simply places a clear direction on your heart, **Arise. Go. Move forward.** These moments may feel subtle, but they carry the same weight as the commands you once followed in uniform. They are invitations to step into something new, something purposeful, something shaped by His hand rather than your comfort.

That forward movement may call you to take a step of faith you've been putting off, to let go of old baggage that has slowed you down for years, to finally forgive someone who wounded you deeply, or to start something new that feels bigger than your abilities. It might mean trusting God with a dream that scares you, or responding to a calling that has been quietly tugging at your heart. Each of these steps requires courage, not the loud, dramatic kind, but the steady courage of obedience.

Standing still feels safer. It feels controlled, predictable, and familiar. But God has not called you to stay in place, stuck in old patterns or held back by fear. He has called you to advance, to keep moving, growing, healing, and stepping into the future He is shaping for you. When God says "move," it's because He's already prepared the ground ahead.

Trust His command. Take the step. Advance.

Prayer:
Lord, give me the courage to move when You say go. Lead me into Your purpose.

Call to Action:

What is one step forward God is asking of you?

_____

_____

_____

_____

_____

Day 79: The Power of Remembrance

Scripture: *Remember his marvellous works that he hath done.   Psalm 105:5*

Veterans remember, sometimes more vividly than they'd like. Certain memories stir a deep sense of pride, reminding you of moments when you stood strong, served well, or accomplished something meaningful. Other memories carry pain, the kind that sits quietly in the background of your mind. Some memories bring a smile or even laughter as you recall people, moments, or unexpected situations that lightened the load. And still others carry a heaviness that words can't fully express. Memory is part of a veteran's life, shaping who you are and how you see the world.

But Scripture invites you to elevate your remembrance even higher, not to ignore your past, but to remember something greater running through it: **the faithfulness of God.** When you look back through the years, you'll find moments when His protection was unmistakable, even if you didn't recognize it at the time. You'll see the times He healed you physically or emotionally, restoring things you thought were lost. You'll recall seasons when He provided exactly what you needed, strength, resources, clarity, or help, right when you needed it most. You'll remember how He carried you through sickness, stress, fear, loss, and confusion, keeping you upright when you felt like you were falling apart. And you'll see how He gave you strength in those moments when your own reserves were completely gone.

This kind of remembrance strengthens your faith because it reveals that God has been present all along, before the battles, during them, and after them. Looking back with gratitude builds hope for the days ahead. It reminds you that the God who sustained you then is the same God who sustains you now.

So look back, not to reopen old wounds or relive old chapters, but to recognize God's steady hand woven into the fabric of your story. Every memory reinterpreted through His faithfulness becomes a reminder that you have never walked alone.

Prayer:
God, help me remember Your faithfulness. Strengthen my faith through what You've already done.

Call to Action:

What moment of God's past faithfulness can you recall today?

_____

_____

_____

_____

_____

Day 80: A Veteran's Legacy

Scripture: *A good man leaveth an inheritance to his children's children.   Proverbs 13:22*

Your legacy reaches far beyond the lines printed on your service record. What you accomplished in uniform matters, but the deeper legacy, the one that truly lasts, is written in who you are. It's reflected in your character, in the way you speak to others, in the faith you carry, and in the example you quietly set day after day. Long after medals fade and paperwork is stored away, your life continues to influence the people who watch you, learn from you, and follow your lead.

Your children, and the generations that come after them, will draw strength from the way you live. They may never fully know the sacrifices you made, but they will feel the impact of your choices. Your faith leaves a mark that encourages them to seek God when life feels uncertain. Your integrity leaves a mark that teaches them to stand firm in truth. Your perseverance leaves a mark that shows them how to endure hardship with courage and dignity. And your prayers leave a mark that surrounds them with spiritual covering long after your words are spoken.

Even on the days when you feel invisible, tired, or unsure if you're making a difference, you are still shaping a legacy. Every act of kindness, every moment of self-control, every decision to forgive, every prayer whispered in quiet places, all of these are seeds planted for the next generation to harvest.

Live today with those future faces in mind. Your legacy is unfolding one day at a time, and God is using even the

smallest moments to build something lasting and beautiful through your life.

Prayer:
Lord, help me build a legacy that honors You and blesses my family for generations.

Call to Action:

What legacy-building action can you take today?

_____

_____

_____

_____

_____

Day 81: When You Need a Reset

Scripture: *Create in me a clean heart, O God, and renew a right spirit within me.   Psalm 51:10*

Sometimes life reaches a point where a reset becomes necessary, a deep breath, a pause, a chance to step back and clear the clutter from your mind and spirit. You've likely felt the need for it many times: a mental reset to quiet the noise, a spiritual reset to realign your heart with God, a simple moment where the frustrations, failures, and fatigue of recent days get wiped away so you can begin again. Veterans especially know what it's like to carry layers of stress without realizing how heavy they've become until everything feels tight inside.

But God specializes in renewal. He doesn't just patch you up or offer temporary relief, He brings real, lasting reset to the places that have grown worn down. He knows how to reset your heart when emotions feel tangled or weighed down. He can reset your attitude when negativity, impatience, or discouragement start taking root. He resets your spirit by breathing fresh strength, clarity, and peace into the places where you feel drained. And He can reset your direction when you feel stuck, uncertain, or unsure which way to move next.

The beautiful part is this: you don't have to wait for a crisis or a breaking point to ask for a fresh start. God doesn't require desperation before He offers renewal. Every new day is an open invitation to begin again with a clear mind and a restored spirit. Renewal is part of His nature, and He delights in giving it freely.

So ask Him to renew you today. Whether you feel worn down or just slightly out of sync, let Him bring the reset your soul needs. God is ready to refresh you long before you reach your limit.

Prayer:
Father, reset my heart and renew my spirit. Restore what life has worn down.

Call to Action:

What attitude or mindset needs a reset?

_____

_____

_____

_____

_____

Day 82: The Call to Stand

Scripture: *Put on the whole armour of God, that ye may be able to stand against the wiles of the devil.*
Ephesians 6:11

Sometimes God calls you to advance, to take new ground, to move boldly into the next step of your journey. But other times, just as importantly, He calls you simply to **stand**. Standing may not look as dramatic as marching forward, but it requires its own kind of strength, resolve, and faith. It is one of the most powerful things a believer can do when the pressure rises.

Stand when you're tired and everything in you wants to collapse.
Stand when the enemy whispers lies that try to undermine your worth, your faith, or your hope.
Stand when temptation pushes hard against your weakest places.
Stand when fear rises and tries to dictate your decisions.
Stand when uncertainty clouds your vision and the path ahead feels unclear.
Stand when your strength feels low, and you aren't sure how much longer you can hold out.

Standing is not passive, it is spiritual warfare. It is a declaration of faith in the face of pressure. It is you planting your feet and saying, **"I will not be moved. God is my anchor, and I refuse to retreat."** When you stand, you resist the enemy. When you stand, you trust God's timing. When you stand, you silence fear. When you stand, you allow God to fight on your behalf.

And the beautiful truth is this: God equips you to hold your ground. He gives you the strength, the armor, the endurance, and the courage to remain steady until the storm finally passes. You are not standing alone, He stands with you, beside you, and within you.

Stand firm today. The battle you're facing is temporary, but the victory God is shaping in you is eternal.

Prayer:
Lord, help me stand firm in Your strength and hold my ground today.

Call to Action:

Where do you need to stand firm today?

_____

_____

_____

_____

_____

Day 83: When God Speaks Through Peace

Scripture: *And let the peace of God rule in your hearts. Colossians 3:15*

Veterans learn to trust many things, your instincts, your training, your awareness, and your ability to read a situation long before anything is spoken. Those skills kept you alive, kept your unit safe, and shaped the way you navigate the world even now. But in your spiritual life, God introduces a different kind of guidance, one that doesn't rely on adrenaline, vigilance, or learned reactions. He teaches you to trust **peace**.

Peace isn't just a pleasant feeling or a moment of calm; it's one of the primary ways God speaks to His people. Peace can serve as His confirmation, settling your spirit when you're heading in the right direction. Peace can also function as His warning, disappearing the moment something is off course. Peace can be His direction, nudging you toward a decision or away from one. And peace can be His presence itself, an inner steadiness that reminds you He is near.

When something steals your peace, that's not something to ignore. It's an invitation to pause, to reconsider, to step back long enough to ask God what He's showing you. And when a decision brings a deep, quiet peace, when your spirit feels aligned and your heart feels settled, that is often God's way of gently saying, "Move forward. I'm in this."

Peace is not just an emotion you feel in good moments; it is a compass God places inside your spirit. It points you

toward wisdom, truth, and safety. It keeps you steady when circumstances shake. It reminds you that you don't have to navigate life on instinct alone, you can trust the One who sees what you cannot.

Let peace rule your heart. Let it shape your choices. Let it steady you in moments of uncertainty. God's peace is reliable, directional, and powerful, and when you follow it, you will not be led astray.

Prayer:
Jesus, let Your peace guide my decisions today. Rule in my heart.

Call to Action:

Which decision requires you to follow God's peace?

_____

_____

_____

_____

_____

Day 84: When You Struggle to Pray

Scripture: *The Spirit itself maketh intercession for us.*
Romans 8:26

There are days when the words simply won't come, when your heart feels too heavy, your mind feels too foggy, or your body feels too exhausted to form a single coherent sentence. Days when life has drained you so deeply that even trying to pray feels overwhelming. Days when you sit before God and all you can offer is silence because you don't even know where to begin or what to ask. Veterans know this feeling well, because carrying so much for so long eventually takes a toll.

But God understands those wordless days more than you realize. He isn't disappointed when your prayers are quiet, incomplete, or tangled. He doesn't wait for polished sentences or impressive spiritual language. Instead, He meets you right in the stillness. And even more comforting, **the Holy Spirit prays for you**. He intercedes on your behalf with perfect understanding, powerful compassion, and intimate knowledge of what your heart needs. He speaks the prayers you can't form. He carries the burdens you can't express. He stands in the gap when you feel emptied out.

You are never truly prayerless, not even for a moment, because the Spirit Himself continues the conversation when your voice grows faint.

So let your silence become a form of worship. Let your tears become prayers that rise to heaven without a single

word attached. Let your sighs, the ones born from stress, fatigue, grief, or longing, become petitions God receives with tenderness. He hears every unspoken ache, every quiet cry, every weary breath.

Nothing you feel is lost on Him. Even when you can't speak a single word, God hears it all.

Prayer:
Holy Spirit, pray for me when I cannot find the words. Strengthen my heart in the quiet.

Call to Action:

What silent prayer will you offer God right now?

_____

_____

_____

_____

_____

Day 85: The Veteran's Compassion

Scripture: *Bear ye one another's burdens.   Galatians 6:2*

Veterans carry a kind of compassion that is shaped by real experience, not theory, not imagination, but lived reality. You have seen pain up close. You've known struggle in ways most people never will. You've endured hardship, loss, exhaustion, and moments that left lasting marks on your mind and heart. And yet, rather than becoming hardened or numb, many veterans discover that these experiences have softened them, made them more aware of the suffering of others, more patient with people's weaknesses, and more understanding of battles that aren't always visible.

God wants to use that compassion. He placed it in you not just as a result of your past, but as a tool for your present. There are people around you right now, family members carrying silent stress, coworkers dealing with private pressures, church members facing spiritual battles, and other veterans who feel unseen or misunderstood, who need exactly what you carry. Your strength brings stability to those who feel shaken. Your patience offers comfort to the overwhelmed. Your empathy gives permission for others to finally breathe and feel safe enough to open up.

When you take the time to listen, to encourage, to lift someone's burden even a little, you reflect Christ more clearly than many sermons ever could. Scripture says that bearing one another's burdens fulfills the law of Christ, and your compassion makes that possible in a powerful way. The kindness you show, the support you offer, and the

understanding you bring aren't small gestures, they are ministry in its purest form.

Your compassion is not accidental. It's not leftover emotion from another season. It is a calling, a gift, and a powerful reflection of Jesus working through your life. Let God continue to use it. Others need what He has placed in you.

Prayer:
Lord, give me eyes to see who needs compassion today. Help me carry their burdens with love.

Call to Action:

Who needs compassion from you today?

_____

_____

_____

_____

_____

Day 86: When God Redirects Your Path

Scripture: *The steps of a good man are ordered by the Lord.   Psalm 37:23*

In the military, you learned early on that routes could change at a moment's notice. Plans that seemed solid were suddenly rewritten. Orders were updated without explanation, and missions shifted with little warning. You adapted because you had to, trusting that those giving the commands saw a bigger picture, one you weren't always privy to. Flexibility became part of your strength, and learning to move with changing circumstances became second nature.

God often redirects your life in much the same way. A door that once looked promising closes unexpectedly. A new opportunity shows up before you feel ready. Your direction shifts in a way you didn't plan. A sense of calling changes shape. A detour appears out of nowhere, throwing off what you thought your path would look like. These moments can feel disruptive or confusing, but they are never random. They are the careful adjustments of a perfect Commander who sees every threat, every obstacle, every possibility, and every blessing, long before you do.

You may not always understand why things change. The detours might feel inconvenient, the delays frustrating, and the redirections puzzling. But the One who leads you doesn't make careless decisions. Every change He allows is connected to your protection or your purpose. Sometimes He reroutes you to shield you from harm you never knew

was coming. Other times He shifts your direction so He can guide you into something better than what you had planned.

You don't have to fully understand the path to trust the One who maps it out. God's redirection is always intentional, always wise, and always rooted in His deep love for you. Every shift in your journey is leading you exactly where He wants you to be.

Prayer:
Father, guide my steps and redirect my path wherever You choose. Help me trust Your leading.

Call to Action:

Where might God be redirecting your steps?

_____

_____

_____

_____

_____

Day 87: Confidence in the Commander

Scripture: *The Lord is my shepherd; I shall not want. Psalm 23:1*

Confidence in leadership was foundational during your service. When you had a commander you trusted, one who was steady, competent, and clear, you found confidence not only in the mission, but in your ability to carry it out. A strong leader could steady your nerves in chaos, give direction when the situation became uncertain, and instill courage simply through their presence. Leadership shaped morale, shaped trust, and shaped how you moved forward.

Spiritually, Jesus occupies that role in an even deeper and more perfect way. He is both your Commander and your Shepherd, faithful in every season, wise beyond measure, protective over every step, and unshakably present in every circumstance. His leadership doesn't falter. His guidance never comes from incomplete information. His commands are never careless or rushed. He knows the terrain ahead, understands the threats you can't see, and prepares you for challenges long before you encounter them.

Because He leads you, you lack nothing truly essential. He provides strength, direction, peace, and provision exactly when you need it. You are never abandoned, not in confusion, not in hardship, not in exhaustion, and not in moments when you feel spiritually dry. His guidance is constant, whether you feel it clearly or only notice it in hindsight. His covering is over your mind, your heart, your home, and your steps.

So follow Him with the same confidence you once placed in leaders you respected, yet with even greater assurance, because Jesus will never misjudge a situation, never lead you into unnecessary danger, and never ask you to walk alone. He will never mislead you. His leadership is perfect, and His heart for you is steady, strong, and true.

Prayer:
Lord, help me trust You completely as my Leader, Shepherd, and Commander.

Call to Action:

What worry do you need to place under Christ's leadership?

_____

_____

_____

_____

_____

Day 88: Training for Eternity

Scripture: *Exercise thyself rather unto godliness.*
1 Timothy 4:7

Your military training shaped you in profound ways, your discipline, your resilience, your mindset, your ability to endure hardship, and your confidence under pressure. It influenced how you think, how you act, and how you respond when challenges rise. That training had a lifelong impact on your character. But as powerful as that formation was, your spiritual training reaches even farther. It doesn't just shape your years on earth, it shapes your eternity.

Every prayer you pray strengthens your inner life, teaching your heart to depend on God more than on your own strength. Every act of obedience, big or small, builds spiritual maturity, forming Christlike character that lasts. Every time you open Scripture, your heart is being equipped with truth that anchors you, corrects you, protects you, and guides your steps. Every moment of worship deepens your connection with God, softening your spirit and aligning you with His presence. And every small act of faith, whether trusting God with a decision, forgiving someone who hurt you, or stepping out into something new, prepares you for the eternal rewards God promises His people.

You're not just training for today. You're not just preparing for the next battle or the next season. Every spiritual discipline, every step of obedience, every moment spent with God is shaping who you become for eternity. This training isn't temporary, and the rewards aren't fleeting. You are being formed for something far greater than this life can show you.

So keep training. Keep growing. Keep sharpening your spirit the way you once sharpened your skills in uniform. The work you do in your spirit now echoes into forever. And eternity, glorious, joyful, unshakeable, awaits you.

Prayer:
Lord, help me train for godliness with the same discipline I once trained as a soldier.

Call to Action:

What spiritual "training" will you practice today?

_____

_____

_____

_____

_____

Day 89: The Power of Blessing

Scripture: *Death and life are in the power of the tongue.*
Proverbs 18:21

Your words carry far more weight than you may realize. As a veteran, your voice carries a natural authority born from experience, people listen when you speak because they sense the strength, discipline, and credibility behind your words. You've lived through situations that shaped your perspective, and that gives your voice a presence that others instinctively respect. Whether you speak quietly or boldly, what you say has the power to shift the tone of a room and impact the hearts of the people around you.

Because of that, God calls you to use your voice intentionally. Speak life into the weary, reminding them that their story isn't finished. Speak encouragement into those who doubt themselves or feel overwhelmed. Speak truth into situations clouded by confusion or fear. Speak hope into people who feel like they're running out of it. And above all, speak Christ, His love, His grace, His wisdom, and His comfort.

Your words aren't small or insignificant. They can change atmospheres, lift spirits, heal wounds that aren't visible, and strengthen souls that feel close to breaking. A single sentence from you might be exactly what someone needs to keep going, someone in your family, your workplace, your church, or even another veteran fighting a silent battle.

So speak blessing today. Let your words reflect the warrior of God you've become, steady, compassionate, truthful, and full of hope. Your voice is a gift. Use it to build, to uplift, and to point others toward the One who gives life.

Prayer:
Lord, use my words to bring life, strength, and hope to others.

Call to Action:

Who can you speak life and encouragement to today?

_____

_____

_____

_____

_____

Day 90: The Mission Continues

Scripture: *Well done, good and faithful servant.*
Matthew 25:23

Your military service may now be a completed chapter, but your Kingdom service continues with every breath you take. The uniform may be folded away, but the calling God has placed on your life remains active, meaningful, and eternal. Your mission today reaches far beyond earthly ranks or earthly assignments. It touches hearts, shapes futures, and impacts eternity.

Your mission now is to love deeply, offering compassion, patience, and grace in a world that desperately needs it. It is to serve faithfully in whatever role God places before you, whether visible or unseen. It is to walk in integrity, showing the world what Christlike character looks like in everyday decisions. It is to fight spiritual battles with prayer, endurance, and truth, recognizing that your enemy is not flesh and blood. It is to raise your family in faith, leaving a legacy of hope and devotion that outlives you. It is to share your testimony, reminding others that God works through every chapter of your story, both the victories and the valleys. It is to build others up, strengthening those who feel weak or overlooked. And it is to follow Christ wholeheartedly, trusting Him as your true Commander.

One day, when your final mission on earth is complete, you will stand before the Lord, and you will hear the words every veteran longs to hear from the One who leads

perfectly and loves completely: **"Well done."** That moment will make every sacrifice worth it.

Until that day, stand strong. Walk faithfully. Carry out your mission with the courage, discipline, and devotion that have always defined you. Your service to God's Kingdom is not finished, it's ongoing, powerful, and deeply needed. Continue the mission with the confidence that He goes before you every step of the way.

Prayer:
Lord, thank You for 90 days of drawing me closer to You. Strengthen me for the mission ahead.

Call to Action:

What is the next spiritual mission God is calling you into?

_____

_____

_____

_____

_____

www.ingramcontent.com/pod-product-compliance
Lightning Source LLC
LaVergne TN
LVHW051405080426
835508LV00022B/2978